Connect *with* **English**

CONVERSATION BOOK 1

Pam Tiberia
Janet Battiste
Michael Berman
Linda Butler

McGraw-Hill

Boston, Massachusetts   Burr Ridge, Illinois   Dubuque, Iowa   Madison, Wisconsin
New York, New York   San Francisco, California   St. Louis, Missouri
Bangkok   Bogotá   Caracas   Lisbon   London   Madrid   Mexico City
Milan   New Delhi   Seoul   Singapore   Sydney   Taipei   Toronto

McGraw-Hill

A Division of The **McGraw·Hill** *Companies*

CONNECT WITH ENGLISH: CONVERSATION BOOK 1

This book is printed on acid-free paper.

domestic   6 7 8 9 0 DOW DOW 9 0 01 0 2 03
international 1 2 3 4 5 6 7 8 9 DOW DOW 9 0 0 9 8 7

ISBN 0-07-292764-X

Editorial director: Thalia Dorwick
Publisher: Tim Stookesberry
Development editor: Pam Tiberia
Marketing manager: Tracy Landrum
Production supervisor: Richard DeVitto
Print materials consultant: Marilyn Rosenthal
Project manager: Gayle Jaeger, Function Thru Form, Inc.
Design and Electronic Production: Function Thru Form, Inc.
Typeface: Frutiger
Printer and Binder: R. R. Donnelley & Sons

Grateful acknowledgment is made for use of the following:

Still Photography: Jeffrey Dunn, Ron Gordon, Judy Mason, Margaret Strom

***Additional Photographs: Episode 1** – page 1 left to right, top:* © A. Archer/Shooting Star, © Richard Aaron/ Shooting Star, © R. Drechsler/Shooting Star, © Glen A. Baker/Shooting Star; *bottom:* © Marc Morrison/Shooting Star, © J. Henry Fair/Retna Ltd; ***Episode 5** – page 1 left to right, top:* © Kevin Horan/Stock Boston, © Dick Reed/The Stock Market, © 88 Swarthout & Assoc./The Stock Market; *bottom:* © David Burnett/Contact Press Images/The Stock Market, © Super Stock, © Super Stock; ***Episode 6** – page 7 left to right:* © Bill Horsman/Stock Boston, © John Coletti/Stock Boston; ***Episode 10** – page 4:* © Michael Newman/PhotoEdit; ***Episode 11** – pages 5 and 6, first column:* © Erik Heinila/Shooting Star, © S.S.Archives/Shooting Star; *second column:* © NBC/Shooting Star, © Marc Morrison/ Shooting Star; *third column:* © Photofest, © Raul de Molina/Shooting Star, © Photofest; *fourth column:* © Jan Hoffmann/Shooting Star, © S.S.Archives/Shooting Star, © Joan Alden/Shooting Star; *page 7 top to bottom:* © Tom Bean/Tony Stone Images, © Tom Ulrich/Tony Stone Images, © Super Stock, © William J. Herbert/Tony Stone Images

***Illustrations: Episode 2** – page 1:* Steve Stankiewicz; *page 2:* George Riemann; ***Episode 3** – page 3:* Steve Stankiewicz; *page 6:* Bob Schuchman; ***Episode 4** – page 1:* Lisa Goldrick; *pages 2 and 4:* Amy Wummer; *pages 5 and 6:* Andrew Shiff; ***Episode 5** – page 3:* Steve Stankiewicz; *page 4:* Amy Wummer; *page 6:* Chris Duke; ***Episode 6** – page 2:* Steve Stankiewicz; ***Episode 7** – pages 2 and 6:* Steve Stankiewicz; *page 3:* Nick Jainschigg; ***Episode 8** – page 1:* Lisa Goldrick; *page 4:* Amy Wummer; ***Episode 9** – page 4:* George Riemann; *pages 5 and 6:* Andrew Shiff; ***Episode 10** – page 1:* Amy Wummer; *page 3 top:* George Riemann; *page 3 bottom, and page 6:* Steve Stankiewicz; ***Episode 11** – page 3:* George Riemann; ***Episode 12** – page 1:* Steve Stankiewicz; ***Appendices 7 and 13** –* Steve Stankiewicz

Special thanks to Deborah Gordon, Robin Longshaw, Cheryl Pavlik, and Bill Preston for their contributions to *Conversation Books 1–4.*

Library of Congress Catalog Card No.: 97-75580

http://www.mhhe.com

Table of Contents

	THEMES	TWO-PAGE ACTIVITY	OPTIONAL PROJECT
EPISODE 1 *REBECCA'S DREAM*	• Favorite Songs • Pursuing Your Dreams • Male/Female Relationships	SONG: TRAVELING LIGHT	Choosing a College *(Appendix 1)*
EPISODE 2 *DIFFERENCES*	• Making a Shopping List • Taking Care of Someone • Friendship	INFORMATION GAP: SAVING MONEY	Working in a Factory *(Appendix 2)*
EPISODE 3 *A VISIT TO THE DOCTOR*	• Going to the Doctor • Career Choices • Barbecues	GAME: WHAT'S YOUR JOB?	Holidays *(Appendix 3)*
EPISODE 4 *CELEBRATIONS*	• Expressing Congratulations • Graduation from High School • Getting Accepted	INFORMATION GAP: DIFFERENT TYPES OF FAMILIES	Being Proud *(Appendix 4)*
EPISODE 5 *BREAKING THE NEWS*	• Buying a Used Car • A Shopping Mall • Formal and Informal Clothes	GAME: A PARENT'S APPROVAL	Shopping for Clothes *(Appendix 5)*
EPISODE 6 *SAYING GOODBYE*	• Saying Goodbye to Friends • Music Lessons • Junk Food	INFORMATION GAP: BASEBALL	The Boston Red Sox *(Appendix 6)*

To the Teacher

The primary goal of each *Conversation Book* is to help students develop oral communication skills using the themes found in **Connect with English** as a springboard for classroom discussion. This introduction and the following Visual Tour provide important information on how each *Conversation Book* and the corresponding video episodes can be successfully combined to teach English as a second or foreign language.

LANGUAGE SKILLS:

Each *Conversation Book* has 12 chapters which contain a variety of pair, group, team, and whole-class activities that are based on important issues and ideas from the corresponding video episodes.

The activity types vary with each chapter but generally include an assortment of role-plays, discussions, opinion surveys, games, interviews, and question-naires. In each chapter, a special two-page section is devoted to longer games, information gaps, and songs from the **Connect with English** sound-track. Students also have the opportunity to work on special project pages found in appendices in the back of the book. These projects provide students with the opportunity to explore key themes outside of the classroom.

THEMATIC ORGANIZATION:

Events and issues that are familiar and important to all ESL/EFL learners have been purposely included in the **Connect with English** story. These topics were carefully chosen for their relevant cultural content, and they provide a rich context for the communicative activities found in the *Conversation Books.* As students watch the video story and become familiar with the events and characters, the *Conversation Books* provide a framework within which students can freely discuss the ideas presented in each episode. Throughout *Conversation Books 1-4,* students are given the opportunity to explore such varied themes as the following:

- Pursuing Your Dream
- Making Future Plans
- Looking for a Job
- Making New Friends
- Money vs. Love
- Having Fun
- Apologizing
- Making a Difficult Decision
- Gossip
- Divorce and Remarriage
- Regrets
- Anger

- Making Compromises
- Spending Money
- Adulthood
- Best Friends
- Managing Priorities
- Parenting
- Helping Others
- The Death of a Loved One
- Dedication
- Moving
- Holidays
- Life Lessons

PROFICIENCY LEVEL:

The activities found in each *Conversation Book* are designed for use with high-beginning to intermediate students. Special icons are used to identify the difficulty level of each activity in the book. These icons help teachers tailor the activities for the needs of students at different levels of language proficiency.

 Arrows pointing up indicate that the difficulty of an activity can be increased.

 Arrows pointing down indicate that an activity can be simplified.

 Arrows pointing in both directions indicate that the difficulty level of the activity can be either increased or simplified.

Detailed teaching suggestions on modifying each activity are found in the accompanying Instructor's Manual.

OPTIONS FOR USE:

The *Conversation Books* are specifically designed for classroom use. While it is assumed that students have watched the corresponding video episode at least once before attempting the activities in the book, it is not necessary to have classroom access to a TV or VCR. Teachers may choose to show the video during class time, or they can assign students to watch the video episodes prior to class, either in a library, language lab, or at home. Class time can then be used for completion of the activities found in the *Conversation Book.*

Each *Conversation Book* can be used as the sole text in any course that emphasizes oral communication skills. Teachers also have the option of combining the *Conversation Books* with other corresponding texts in the **Connect with English** print package:

■ *Video Comprehension Books 1-4* contain a variety of comprehension activities that enhance and solidify students' understanding of main events in the video story.

■ *Grammar Guides 1-4* provide multilevel practice in grammar structures and vocabulary items derived from the **Connect with English** video episodes.

■ *Connections Reader Series* (16 titles) offer students graded reading practice based on the **Connect with English** story.

■ *Video Scripts 1-4* include the exact dialogue from each of the video episodes and can be used in a variety of ways in conjunction with any of the other texts in the **Connect with English** program.

For additional information on these and other materials in the **Connect with English** program, please refer to the inside back cover of this book.

A VISUAL TOUR OF THIS TEXT

This visual tour is designed to introduce the key features of *Conversation Book 1*. The primary focus of each *Conversation Book* is to help students develop oral communication skills within the context of the **Connect with English** story. *Conversation Book 1* corresponds to episodes 1–12 of **Connect with English**, and it presents an assortment of activities dealing with various aspects of communication, including explaining, questioning, interviewing, reporting, paraphrasing, describing, stating feelings/opinions, and more.

Themes drawn directly from the video episodes are listed at the start of each chapter. In Episode 7, activities are based on the themes of Surprises, Presents, and Good Luck/Bad Luck. A two-page game is devoted to Rebecca's trip across the U.S., and an optional project offers students an opportunity to become more familiar with the United States.

A regular feature of the *Conversaton Books*, **Ways to Say It** activities introduce students to several common expressions used in daily conversation. Special effort has been made to include high-frequency, natural language which reflects the language used in the video episodes and in everyday speech in the United States and Canada.

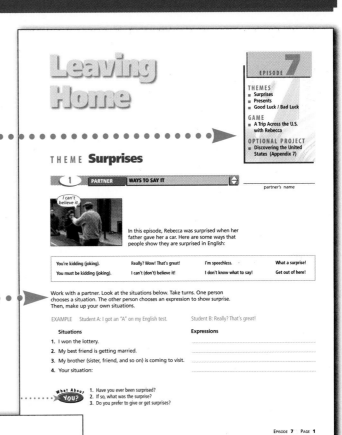

Multilevel Activities

Special icons are used to show the difficulty level of each activity in the book. These icons are designed to help teachers tailor the activities for the needs of a multilevel group of students. An arrow pointing up ▼ indicates that the difficulty of an activity can be increased, while an arrow pointing down ▲ indicates that an activity can be simplified for lower-level students. Arrows pointing in both directions ◆ indicate that the activity can be adjusted in either direction. Detailed teaching suggestions for how to change the level of each activity in *Conversation Book 1* are included in the accompanying Instructor's Manual.

Activity bars identify the start of each numbered activity and indicate whether the activity is designed for pairs, groups, teams, or whole-class participation. Descriptors such as **Discussion, Interview,** or **Role-Play** alert teachers to the type of activity that follows.

Variety of Activity Types

Each chapter contains a variety of activity types that feature different student combinations and communicative objectives. For example, Activity 3 on this page features teams competing in a timed categorizing game, while Activity 4 asks partners to perform a role-play involving the purchase of a gift.

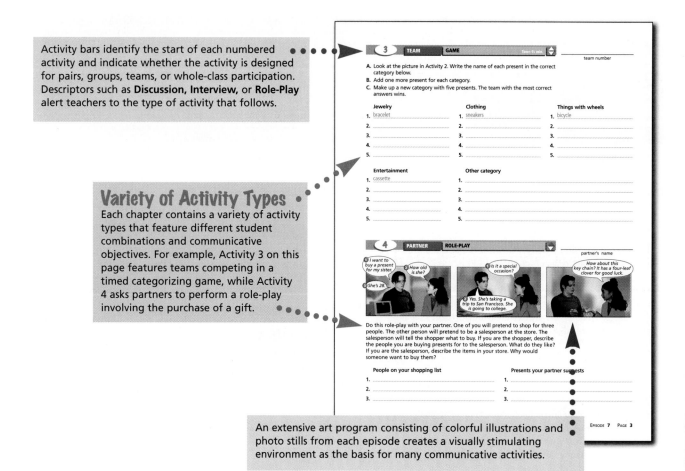

An extensive art program consisting of colorful illustrations and photo stills from each episode creates a visually stimulating environment as the basis for many communicative activities.

Activities such as group discussions and opinion surveys invite students to share personal experiences and opinions as they relate to the themes from the video story. In Activity 5, students compare ideas about symbols of good and bad luck.

Conversation Book 1 often features a logical progression of activities. For example, a group survey on superstition in Activity 6 is followed by an analysis of the data in Activity 7. This organization reinforces important concepts and vocabulary and provides an additional opportunity to discuss various issues evolving from each theme.

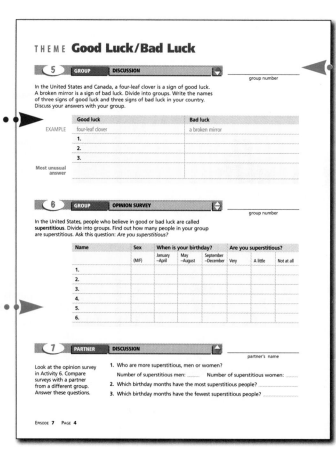

Spaces that allow students to indicate partner name, group number, and team number make it easier for students and teachers to keep track of student collaborations. Group and team numbers are also useful when different groups are asked to compare and contrast survey or discussion results with one another.

Two-Page Activity

Each episode contains an extended theme which is covered in a longer, two-page activity. These themes are developed into games, information gaps, or activities based on songs from the *Connect with English* soundtrack.

This two-page game, "A Trip Across the U.S. with Rebecca," centers on Rebecca's trip from Boston to San Francisco. In this game, students are involved in the creation of the game questions. This participation simultaneously increases motivation and reviews important concepts and vocabulary related to the story.

Step-by-step explanations and clear, concise examples provide necessary structure and format as students prepare and create game cards. Game instructions are presented in an organized fashion that takes students through each step of play.

GAME A Trip Across the U.S. with Rebecca

8 | **TEAM** | **GAME**

team number

In this episode, Rebecca is going to leave Boston and drive to San Francisco. Play this game, and cross the United States with Rebecca. The team that gets to California first wins.

Get Ready to Play

Step One

Divide into four teams. Each team writes 20 questions and answers about the story so far. Work with your team to write five questions and answers for each of the categories below. Use your own paper.

	Who?	What?	Where?	Why?
EXAMPLE	Who plays the guitar? (Rebecca)	What is the name of Rebecca's brother? (Kevin)	Where is Rebecca going to college? (San Francisco)	Why does Rebecca leave home? (She wants to go to college.)
	1.	1.	1.	1.
	2.	2.	2.	2.
	3.	3.	3.	3.
	4.	4.	4.	4.
	5.	5.	5.	5.

Step Two

After your teacher checks your team's questions and answers, copy the questions on separate pieces of paper (or index cards). Write the questions and your team's number on the front. Write the answers on the back.

Step Three

Cut out the die and the other game pieces on Appendix 13. Each team should pick one car and one game marker.

FRONT

Team 1
Who plays the guitar?

Rebecca

BACK

Play the Game

- Each team puts its square marker on the gameboard at **GO** and its car in the state of Massachusetts.
- One player from each team arranges the question cards in four piles—who, what, where, and why. This player will ask the questions for the team seated across from him/her.
- Decide who goes first. Roll the die. The team with the highest number starts, and play continues to the right.
- The first team rolls the die, and moves its marker the number of spaces indicated (if a 2 is rolled, the marker is moved two spaces, and so on).
- If a team lands on a question space (who, what, where, or why), that team member must answer a question from that card pile to move on.
- If the team's answer is correct, the team member is allowed to move the car one state closer to California. He/she gets to roll the die again, and take another turn. If the team's answer is incorrect, that team loses its turn. Play continues to the right with the next team.
- If the team lands on a **DETOUR** space, the team member must move the car to the state that is indicated and lose a turn. On the next turn, he/she will start from that state on his/her way to California.
- The first team to get its car to California wins.

EPISODE **7** PAGE **5**

GAME A Trip Across the U.S. with Rebecca

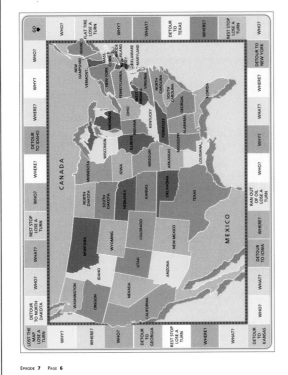

EPISODE **7** PAGE **6**

Each book contains colorful game boards that are removable, making them easy for students to use on a desk or tabletop. Game pieces and markers for students to cut out and use are found in Appendix 13 at the back of the book.

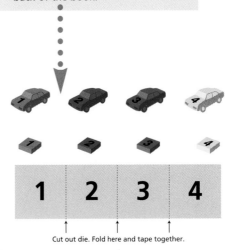

Cut out die. Fold here and tape together.

Project Page

Optional project pages correspond to each episode and are found in appendices located at the back of the book. Project pages contain research-oriented activities or community surveys and polls based on important themes from each episode. These projects reinforce the communicative nature of the *Conversation Books* and invite students to expand their learning and conversation to areas beyond the classroom environment.

On this project page, students discover different regions of the United States. As they gather information, students are often asked to synthesize their findings with those of their classmates in order to gain a complete understanding of the theme. Many times, students will be asked to make a class presentation, which serves the dual purpose of solidifying their own knowledge of the material and successfully communicating it to their classmates.

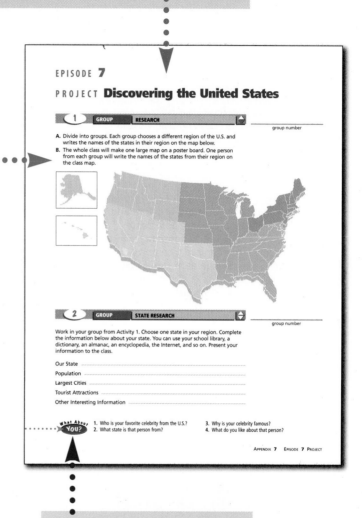

EPISODE **7**

PROJECT **Discovering the United States**

1 GROUP RESEARCH
group number

A. Divide into groups. Each group chooses a different region of the U.S. and writes the names of the states in their region on the map below.
B. The whole class will make one large map on a poster board. One person from each group will write the names of the states from their region on the class map.

2 GROUP STATE RESEARCH
group number

Work in your group from Activity 1. Choose one state in your region. Complete the information below about your state. You can use your school library, a dictionary, an almanac, an encyclopedia, the Internet, and so on. Present your information to the class.

Our State
Population
Largest Cities
Tourist Attractions
Other Interesting Information

What About You?
1. Who is your favorite celebrity from the U.S.?
2. What state is that person from?
3. Why is your celebrity famous?
4. What do you like about that person?

APPENDIX **7** EPISODE **7** PROJECT

What About You? activities provide open-ended questions that encourage students to express their personal feelings, opinions, and reactions to the events and characters in the story. These activities create a springboard for more sophisticated discussions among students who are at higher levels of oral proficiency. **What About You?** activities can also be used as optional writing assignments.

Rebecca's Dream

THEME Favorite Songs

1 GROUP SURVEY

Pop _____

Rock _____

Jazz _____

Step One

Look at the pictures. What's your favorite type of music? Circle your favorite.

Step Two

Divide into groups. Talk about music with your group.

Rap _____

Classical _____

Country _____

A. Vote on your favorite type of music. Write the number of votes for each type of music in the small lines under the pictures.

B. Add up the votes. What's your group's favorite type of music? _____ What type of music does your group like the least? _____

C. Compare your answers with those of another group. Do both groups like and dislike the same types of music? _____

_____
partner's name

Think about your two favorite songs. Who sings (or plays) these songs? What type of music are the songs (pop, rock, jazz, and so on)? Why do you like these songs?

A. Fill in Chart A with your answers. Then, tell your partner about your favorite songs.

B. Your partner will tell you about his/her favorite songs. Write what your partner tells you in Chart B.

C. Do you and your partner both like the same type(s) of music? _____

   Are any of your favorite songs (or singers or musicians) the same? _____

CHART A: YOUR FAVORITE SONGS

Name of song	Singer or musician	Type of music	Why you like it
1.			
2.			

CHART B: YOUR PARTNER'S FAVORITE SONGS

Name of song	Singer or musician	Type of music	Why your partner likes it
1.			
2.			

THEME Pursuing Your Dreams

_____
group number

In this episode, Rebecca tells Kevin about her dream of going to music school.

A. What is *your* dream? Draw a picture of your dream on a separate piece of paper. Do not write your name on it.

B. Fold the paper. Everyone in your group will put his/her paper in a pile.

C. Pick a drawing (not your own) from the pile. Try to guess the person's dream from the drawing. If you can't guess the dream, the person who drew the picture will tell you what it is.

D. Vote on the most interesting dream.

_____ has the most interesting dream.
    (name)

PARTNER | **INTERVIEW**

How important are your dreams? Think about your dream from Activity 3.
What would you do to make your dream come true? What wouldn't you do?

A. Write your answers in the chart below.

B. Interview your partner. Ask these questions:
- *What is your dream?*
- *What would you do to make your dream come true?*
- *What wouldn't you do?*

C. Write your partner's answers in the chart. Did any of your partner's answers surprise you?

	YOUR DREAM		YOUR PARTNER'S DREAM	
	Things you would do	**Things you wouldn't do**	**Things your partner would do**	**Things your partner wouldn't do**
EXAMPLE	go to school	ask someone for money	work two jobs	quit school

THEME Male/Female Relationships

 GROUP | **SURVEY**

group number

In this episode, Rebecca and Matt talk about their relationship. They each want different things. Sometimes people want different things in a relationship.

Interview three women and three men. Write the women's answers in Chart A and the men's answers in Chart B. Ask each person this question: *What two things are most important in a relationship?*

CHART A: WOMEN'S ANSWERS		
Name	**Most important things in a relationship**	
1.	1.	2.
2.	1.	2.
3.	1.	2.

CHART B: MEN'S ANSWERS		
Name	**Most important things in a relationship**	
1.	1.	2.
2.	1.	2.
3.	1.	2.

Work with a partner. Compare the women's and men's answers from your chart in Activity 5. Combine your survey answers in the picture below.

■ Which answers did *both men and women* give? Write these in the *middle* part of the picture.

■ Which answers did *only women* give? Write these answers in the *left* part of the picture.

■ Which answers did *only men* give? Write these in the *right* part of the picture.

When you finish, join another pair and compare your pictures. How are they similar? How are they different?

Women's answers

Men's and women's answers

Men's answers

1. Do you have a good relationship with someone?
2. Do you know many people who have good relationships?
3. Is it hard work to have a good relationship?

Traveling Light

 GROUP | **SONG**

In this episode, Rebecca sings a song about her dream. The name of the song is *Traveling Light*. To **travel light** is an idiom. It means to travel without many things, or to take only the things you really need.

Rebecca wrote the song *Traveling Light*. The words that she wrote are called **lyrics**. Look at Rebecca's song below. Many of the words, or lyrics, are missing. Work with your group to fill in the correct words in the empty spaces.

A. Divide into small groups. Read the lyrics to Rebecca's song.
If you remember any of the missing words, fill them in.

B. Try to guess what the other missing words are.
Write your guesses in the spaces, or at the end of the line.

C. For the remaining words, read the clues in the box.
Fill in the words so that the lyrics are complete.

D. When you are finished, look at the song lyrics on page 6 to check your answers.

Traveling Light

I've got my _____, and I've got my hat.
(1)

I've got my reason to ride.

I've got my _____, but they're
(2)

_____ behind.
(3)

I'm traveling light.

I've got my _____, and I've got my
(4)

_____.
(5)

I've got my reason to ride.

I've got some dreams, I'm going to hold on tight.

I'm _____ light.
(6)

Outside the _____ are slipping by,
(7)

each with its own little light.

Inside the _____ are dreaming,
(8)

just like the dreams I have _____.
(9)

C L U E S

1. a piece of paper which shows you have paid for a trip

2. events and things you remember

3. a long way

4. a large bag or box to carry clothing

5. something warm to wear over your clothing

6. going somewhere

7. places where people live

8. human beings

9. this evening

S O N G **Traveling Light**

 GROUP | **SONG**

Here are the lyrics to Rebecca's song, *Traveling Light*. Check your answers on page 5.

▲▼▲▼▲▼▲▼▲▼▲▼▲▼▲▼▲▼▲▼▲▼▲

Traveling Light

Verse 1
I've got my ticket, and I've got my hat.
I've got my reason to ride.
I've got my memories, but they're far behind.
I'm traveling light.

Verse 2
I've got my suitcase, and I've got my coat.
I've got my reason to ride.
I've got some dreams, I'm going to hold on tight.
I'm traveling light.

Verse 3
Outside the houses are slipping by,
each with its own little light.
Inside the people are dreaming,
just like the dreams I have tonight.

 PARTNER | **WRITING A SONG**

A. Work with a partner. Write one more verse for the song, *Traveling Light*. Think about these questions:
- *Where do you think the person in the song is going?*
- *What is he/she going to do there?*

Use Verses 1 and 2 of the song as examples to help you write. Notice that the last line of each verse ends with the sentence: *I'm traveling light*. Use your imagination. Have fun!

B. When you finish, practice singing your verse together. Then sing or say it for the class.

C. Vote on the best verse. The pair with the most votes wins.

Your verse to *Traveling Light*

_____

_____

_____

_____

Differences

EPISODE **2**

THEMES
- Making a Shopping List
- Taking Care of Someone
- Friendship

INFORMATION GAP
- Saving Money

OPTIONAL PROJECT
- Working in a Factory (Appendix 2)

THEME **Making a Shopping List**

1 | **PARTNER** | **INTERVIEW**

_____
partner's name

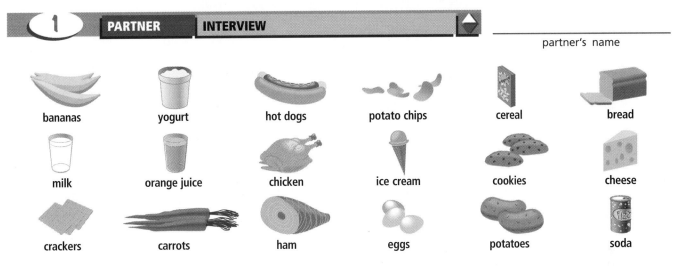

bananas	yogurt	hot dogs	potato chips	cereal	bread
milk	orange juice	chicken	ice cream	cookies	cheese
crackers	carrots	ham	eggs	potatoes	soda

You and your partner are shopping for food.

A. Look at the picture above. Circle five items that you want to buy. Write them on your shopping list below.

B. Write three extra items that you want to buy that are *not* in the picture.

C. Ask your partner these questions:
- *What five items do you want to buy?*
- *What three extra items do you want to buy?*
Write your partner's answers below.

Your shopping list

1. _____
2. _____
3. _____
4. _____
5. _____

Your extra items

1. _____
2. _____
3. _____

Your partner's shopping list

1. _____
2. _____
3. _____
4. _____
5. _____

Your partner's extra items

1. _____
2. _____
3. _____

Your group is having a party. You have enough money to buy six items. Discuss the items you want to buy. Write your shopping list below. Everyone in the group must agree on all of the items on the list.

1. _____   **4.** _____

2. _____   **5.** _____

3. _____   **6.** _____

THEME **Taking Care of Someone**

3 **CLASS** **SURVEY**

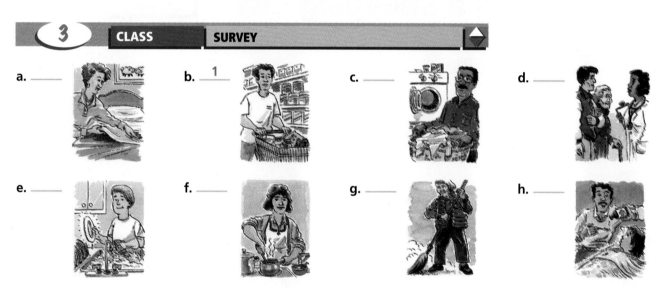

a. _____   b. __1__   c. _____   d. _____

e. _____   f. _____   g. _____   h. _____

Do you take care of someone in your family? Do you take care of a friend? What do you do?

A. Match the pictures above with the activities listed below. Write the number in the space.

B. Put a check (✔) in Column A next to all the things you do.

C. Walk around your class, and find someone who does each activity. Write his/her name in Column B.

Ask this question: *Do you __buy the groceries__?*

ACTIVITY

	COLUMN A	COLUMN B
	Things you do	**Classmates who do these things**
1. buy the groceries		
2. sweep the floor		
3. cook the food		
4. make someone's bed		
5. wash the dishes		
6. give someone his/her medicine		
7. do the laundry		
8. take someone to the doctor		

A. Read the two opinions below. Put a check (✔) next to the opinion you agree with.

B. Your teacher will divide the class into groups of people who have the same opinion. In your group, make a list of at least five reasons why you believe your opinion is true.

C. Each group will read its list of reasons to the class. The rest of the class will ask questions.

D. After all groups have read their reasons, the whole class will vote on the best reason to support each opinion.

_____ *Opinion A:* Rebecca should do all of the housekeeping and shopping for the Casey family.

Reasons

1. _____ **4.** _____

2. _____ **5.** _____

3. _____

_____ *Opinion B:* Rebecca should share the housekeeping and shopping with her father and brother.

Reasons

1. _____ **4.** _____

2. _____ **5.** _____

3. _____

T H E M E **Friendship**

 **5** **CLASS** **DISCUSSION**

As a class, discuss what a good friend always does and what a good friend never does. Write your ideas on the lines in the pictures below. Ask a classmate or your teacher to copy the picture onto the board and write the class's answers for everyone to see.

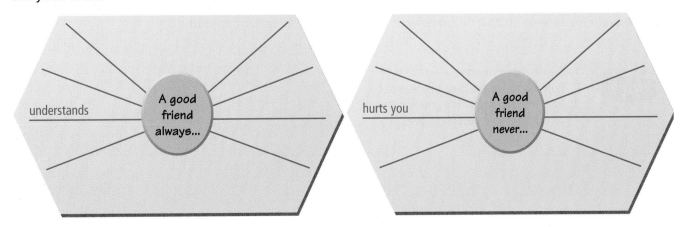

understands — A good friend always...

hurts you — A good friend never...

Take the "Friendship Test" below. Check (✔) *Always*, *Sometimes*, or *Never*. Then ask your partner the questions below, and check (✔) your partner's answers. Add up your scores and discuss your results.

	YOU			YOUR PARTNER		
	Always	Sometimes	Never	Always	Sometimes	Never
1. When friends call, do you always call them back?						
2. Do you ever say mean things about your friends?						
3. Do you help a friend even when you're busy?						
4. Do you call or write to your friends often?						
5. Are you honest with your friends?						
6. Do you really want your friends to succeed?						
7. Do you tell your friends when you're angry at them?						
8. Do you remember your friends' birthdays and other important dates?						
9. Do you listen to your friends' problems and try to help them?						
10. Do you apologize to your friends if you do something to hurt them?						

SCORING: *Always* answers are worth 2 points.
Sometimes answers are worth 1 point.
Never answers are worth 0 points.

If your score is between 16-20 points: You're a great friend!

If your score is between 11-15 points: Sometimes you're a good friend!

If your score is lower than 10 points: Friends are usually not very important to you!

1. Where did you meet your best friend?
2. How long have you been best friends?
3. How often do you talk to your best friend?
4. Where does your best friend live?

INFORMATION GAP **Saving Money**

STUDENT A — Work with a partner. One of you works on this page. The other works on page 6. Don't look at your partner's page.

In this episode, Rebecca saves money to pay for college. With your partner, you will learn about different types of investments (ways to save money). Take turns asking and answering questions about your information. Write the answers in the chart below.

Ask these questions:
1. _How much interest can you earn on a savings account?_
2. _How safe is a savings account?_
3. _Can you take your money out of a savings account at any time?_
4. _How much interest can you earn on a mutual fund?_
5. _How safe is a mutual fund?_
6. _Can you take your money out of a mutual fund at any time?_

Type of investments	Interest percentage (Interest is the amount of money your money earns in an investment.)	How safe is it?	Can you take your money out at any time?
1. Savings Account			
2. 1 Year Certificate of Deposit (CD)	5%	Very safe	Not before one year
3. Mutual Fund (putting money in a group of companies)			
4. Stock (putting money in one company)	15%	Not very safe	Yes

8 | **PARTNER** | **GAME** | Time: 10 min.

_____
partner's name

People save money for different reasons. For example, Rebecca is saving money to pay for her education. With your partner from Activity 7, list all the reasons you can think of to save money. The pair with the most reasons wins.

_____   _____
_____   _____
_____   _____
_____   _____
_____   _____
_____   _____
_____   _____

INFORMATION GAP **Saving Money**

STUDENT B Work with a partner. One of you works on this page. The other works on page 5. Don't look at your partner's page.

In this episode, Rebecca saves money to pay for college. With your partner, you will learn about different types of investments (ways to save money). Take turns asking and answering questions about your information. Write the answers in the chart below.

Ask these questions:

1. _How much interest can you earn on a 1-year certificate of deposit?_
2. _How safe is a CD?_
3. _Can you take your money out of a CD at any time?_
4. _How much interest can you earn on a stock?_
5. _How safe is a stock?_
6. _Can you take your money out of a stock at any time?_

Type of investments	Interest percentage (Interest is the amount of money your money earns in an investment.)	How safe is it?	Can you take your money out at any time?
1. Savings Account	3%	Very safe	Yes
2. 1 Year Certificate of Deposit (CD)			
3. Mutual Fund (putting money in a group of companies)	10%	Somewhat safe	Yes
4. Stock (putting money in one company)			

People save money for different reasons. For example, Rebecca is saving money to pay for her education. With your partner from Activity 7, list all the reasons you can think of to save money. The pair with the most reasons wins.

A Visit to the Doctor

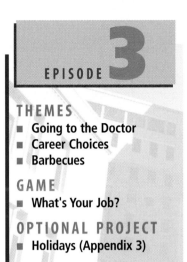

THEME **Going to the Doctor**

1 **GROUP** **CATEGORIES**

group number

doctor	X-ray	receptionist	✔ listens to your heart
take off your clothes	✔ lab technician	checks your blood pressure	explain how you're feeling
needle	get a shot	writes a prescription	✔ stethoscope
✔ open your mouth and say "AHH"	scale	nurse	checks your temperature

What do you see or do at the doctor's office?

A. Put the items from the list above into the four categories. If you don't know what an item is, ask the people in your group or your teacher.

B. Add one item of your own to each category.

	Category 1 Things the doctor uses	Category 2 Things you do at the doctor's	Category 3 People who work in the doctor's office	Category 4 Things the doctor does
EXAMPLE	stethoscope	open your mouth and say "AHH"	lab technician	listens to your heart
	1.	1.	1.	1.
	2.	2.	2.	2.
	3.	3.	3.	3.
	4.	4.	4.	4.

How do you feel about going to the doctor? Check (✔) your answers. Then, ask your partner the questions. Check (✔) your partner's answers. Ask your partner to explain his/her answers.

	YOU			YOUR PARTNER		
	Always	Sometimes	Never	Always	Sometimes	Never
1. Are you nervous when you go to the doctor?						
2. Do you go to the doctor alone?						
3. Do you ask the doctor a lot of questions?						
4. Do you understand what the doctor tells you?						
5. Do you do what the doctor tells you to do?						

THEME **Career Choices**

What's a good job? What job would you like to have? What job wouldn't you like to have?

A. Rate the jobs in the list below from 1 to 8. Write a 1 next to the best job and an 8 next to the worst job.

B. Find out what your partner's answers are. Ask this question: *What did you rate the firefighter?* Write your partner's answers.

C. Tell your partner why you think the jobs you rated 1 and 2 are the best, and why the jobs you rated 7 and 8 are the worst.

Your opinion	The jobs	Your partner's opinion
	firefighter	
	doctor	
	musician	
	secretary	
	taxi driver	
	astronaut	
	cook	
	teacher	

What will Kevin do when he finishes high school? Sit in a circle. One person begins the game by saying, "When Kevin finishes high school, he will be **an actor**." The word "actor" begins with the letter **a**. The next person must think of a job beginning with the letter **b**. That person says, "When Kevin finishes high school, he will be **an actor or a banker**." Each person repeats all the jobs and adds a new one that starts with the next letter of the alphabet. Keep going until someone forgets a job or you reach the end of the alphabet. Play another game and try to think of different jobs.

1. Do you have a job?
2. If so, do you like your job?
3. If not, what job would you like to have?
4. Why would you like to have this job?

THEME Barbecues

5   **TEAM**   **PUZZLE**   Time: 5 min.

_____

team number

Rebecca and some of her friends are planning a surprise birthday party for Sandy. It will be a barbecue at the park. Divide into teams. Look at the list of food for the party below. Read the clues and guess who will bring which food item. The first team to solve the puzzle wins.

Food	Who will bring it?
1. tortilla chips and salsa dip	_____
2. hamburgers and hot dogs	_____
3. tossed salad with dressing	_____
4. iced tea and soda	_____
5. a birthday cake	_____

C L U E S

▶ Joan likes to bake desserts.

▶ Tim loves to eat meat.

▶ Rick loves salsa.

▶ Kim bought cups and glasses.

▶ Connie is a vegetarian.

partner's name

In the United States and Canada, barbecues are very popular summer activities.

A. Look at the list of things that people usually eat at a barbecue. Ask your teacher about any words you don't understand.

B. Have you tried any of these foods? If you have tried a food, check (✔) whether you like it or not. If you haven't tried a food, check (✔) whether you want to try it or not.

C. Find out your partner's answers. Ask this question: *Have you tried hamburgers?* Then ask: *Did you like hamburgers?* or *Do you want to try hamburgers?* Check (✔) your partner's answers.

D. Join another pair. Compare your answers. Have most people tried all of these foods? _____

Do you have similar foods in your country? _____

YES, I HAVE TRIED IT.					NO, I HAVEN'T TRIED IT.			
I like it.		I don't like it.			I want to try it.		No thanks!	
You	Your partner	You	Your partner		You	Your partner	You	Your partner
				hamburgers				
				hot dogs				
				potato chips				
				corn on the cob				
				Boston baked beans				
				potato salad				
				coleslaw				
				watermelon				
				brownies				
				chocolate chip cookies				
				toasted marshmallows				

1. Do people have barbecues in your country? If so, when?
2. Do you like barbecues?
3. Have you ever been to a barbecue like the one Rebecca goes to?

GAME **What's Your Job?**

 TEAM | **GAME**

Play this guessing game to find out what jobs the other team has.

Get Ready to Play

Step One
Divide into teams. Your teacher will assign each person a different number from 1 to 36. Look at page 6 to find out what job matches your number. Don't let anyone on the other team know what your job is!

Step Two
Try to guess the job of a person from the other team. You can ask 20 *Yes/No* questions, but you can only make ONE guess. Plan your questions with your teammates. Use any of the questions below, or write your own.

Play the Game

■ Ask a person from the other team your 20 questions. Check (✔) his/her answers. You may look at the list of jobs on page 6 as you play.

■ When you think you know your partner's job, make a guess. If your guess is wrong, it's your partner's turn. If your guess is correct, write your partner's name next to the job on page 6. Then switch places and answer your partner's questions.

■ When you're finished, return to your team and add up all of the correct guesses. The team with the most correct guesses wins.

		Yes	No			Yes	No
1.	Do you work outdoors?			7.	Do you work with food?		
2.	Do you work in a factory?			8.	Do you work with tools?		
3.	Do you work in an office?			9.	Do you work with machines?		
4.	Do you work alone?			10.	Is your job dangerous?		
5.	Do you work in front of an audience?			11.	Is your job dirty?		
6.	Do you work with customers?			12.	Is your job fun?		

Your own questions: Yes No

13. _____ ? _____ _____

14. _____ ? _____ _____

15. _____ ? _____ _____

16. _____ ? _____ _____

17. _____ ? _____ _____

18. _____ ? _____ _____

19. _____ ? _____ _____

20. _____ ? _____ _____

TEAM   GAME

team number

an electrician

a plumber

a secretary

an architect

an opera singer

an artist

Job	Name		Job	Name
1. mail carrier	_____		**20.** architect	_____
2. baker	_____		**21.** carpenter	_____
3. ballet dancer	_____		**22.** baseball player	_____
4. gardener	_____		**23.** salesclerk	_____
5. teacher	_____		**24.** telephone operator	_____
6. electrician	_____		**25.** bank teller	_____
7. auto mechanic	_____		**26.** hairdresser	_____
8. opera singer	_____		**27.** veterinarian	_____
9. gas station attendant	_____		**28.** army officer	_____
10. nurse	_____		**29.** dentist	_____
11. plumber	_____		**30.** truck driver	_____
12. farm worker	_____		**31.** TV game show host	_____
13. clown	_____		**32.** pilot	_____
14. cowboy	_____		**33.** fisherman	_____
15. artist	_____		**34.** day care provider	_____
16. fashion model	_____		**35.** waiter	_____
17. lawyer	_____		**36.** house painter	_____
18. secretary	_____			
19. supermarket cashier	_____			

a lawyer

a veterinarian

a carpenter

a day care provider

a clown

a bank teller

a salesclerk

a ballet dancer

Celebrations

EPISODE 4

THEMES
- Expressing Congratulations
- Graduation from High School
- Getting Accepted

INFORMATION GAP
- Different Types of Families

OPTIONAL PROJECT
- Being Proud (Appendix 4)

THEME Expressing Congratulations

| 1 | PARTNER | DISCUSSION | ▲ |

partner's name

1. _____ 2. _____ 3. _____ 4. _____

5. _____ 6. _____ 7. _____

In this episode, people congratulate Kevin for graduating from high school. When do you congratulate somebody? Work with a partner. Match the names of the events below with the pictures, and write the words on the lines. Then, add two more events in 6 and 7.

a new baby	a wedding	a new job
a new home	a birthday	

Here are some ways that people express congratulations:

That's great! / That's wonderful!	I'm so happy for you.	Congratulations!	Good going!
I wish you the best.	Good for you!	Well done!	Way to go!	You deserve it.

Divide into groups. Choose one of the events from Activity 1. Practice giving congratulations. Then, present a skit to the class. Use either the expressions from above or some of your own.

EXAMPLE

① I have something to tell you.
② What is it?
① Tom asked me to marry him.
② You're engaged? That's wonderful!
① I'm so happy for you.
② Thank you.

What About YOU?

1. Have you ever received congratulations?
2. Who congratulated you?
3. Why did he/she congratulate you?
4. Has anyone ever sent you a card or letter of congratulations?

THEME **Graduation from High School**

People often use the words below when they talk about high school graduations in the United States and Canada. Ask your teacher about any words that you don't understand. Check (✓) the words that relate to graduations in your school. Then, find out about graduations in your partner's school. Ask this question:
Is / Are there _speeches_ at graduations at your school?

	Your school	Your partner's school			Your school	Your partner's school
1. awards	❑	❑		5. photographs	❑	❑
2. diplomas	❑	❑		6. music	❑	❑
3. caps and gowns	❑	❑		7. yearbooks	❑	❑
4. speeches	❑	❑		8. parties	❑	❑

Students graduating from high school often have traditional activities. For example, in the United States, many students buy class rings, take a class trip, or go to a special dance called a Senior Prom.

A. What three activities are traditional for students graduating from your school?

1. _____

2. _____

3. _____

B. Tell your partner about these activities. Find out what graduating students usually do at your partner's school.

C. What activities are the same? Write them in the *middle* of the picture below. What activities are different? Write your activities on the *left* and your partner's activities on the *right*.

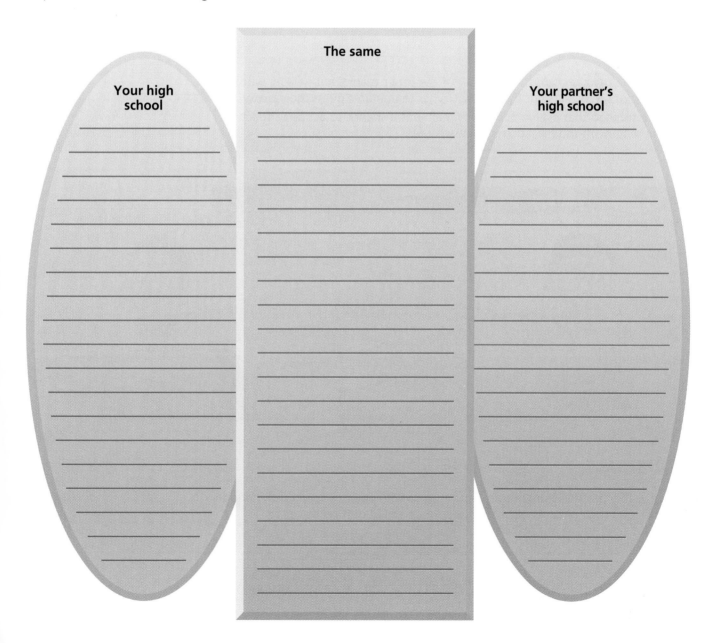

The same

Your high school

Your partner's high school

THEME Getting Accepted

5 TEAM   GAME

_____
team number

A. Divide into teams. Discuss this situation with your teammates:

Imagine you just got accepted to college. What would you do?

Each of you must think of a different reaction. Write each reaction on a piece of paper. These are your reaction cards.

EXAMPLE

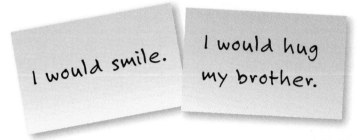

B. Give one reaction card to a member of the other team. That person, who _must not speak_, acts out the words. His/her teammates guess the reaction.
C. Take turns so that everyone on each team has a chance to act out a reaction. The team with the most correct guesses wins.

6 PARTNER   STORYTELLING

_____
partner's name

Work with a partner. Number the pictures in order. Then make up a story about the person in the pictures. Your story should be about getting accepted. Tell your story to the entire class.

What About YOU?
1. Have you ever received a phone call or letter of acceptance?
2. Who was it from?
3. Who is the first person you tell when you get good news?

partner's name

STUDENT **A** Work with a partner. One of you works on this page. The other works on page 6. Don't look at your partner's page.

There are many different types of families in the United States and Canada. Amy's family tree shows you some of them. You and your partner must share information in order to complete the family tree.

A. Ask your partner these questions about Amy's family. Write the answers in the empty spaces in the family tree. Then, answer your partner's questions.

1. What do you know about Amy's great-grandfather?

2. How old is Amy's grandmother?

3. What is the name of Joe's first wife?

4. Who is Tom married to?

5. What is the name of Amy's four-year-old cousin?

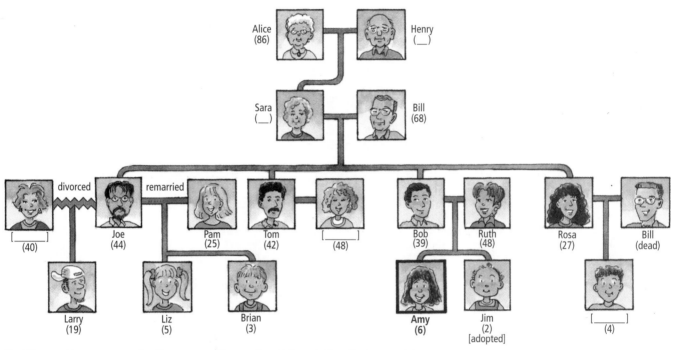

B. Discuss the answers to these questions about Amy's family tree with your partner. Write the answers below.

1. Who are the single (unmarried) mothers? _____

2. Who is married to a much younger woman? _____

3. Which couple has an adopted child? _____

4. Which couple doesn't have any children? _____

5. Who is divorced? _____

 Ask your partner these questions:

1. Do you have a large or small family?

2. Who is the oldest person in your family? The youngest?

3. Is divorce common in your country?

| **PARTNER** | **INFORMATION GAP** | | ⬍ | _____ |

partner's name

STUDENT B Work with a partner. One of you works on this page. The other works on page 5. Don't look at your partner's page.

There are many different types of families in the United States and Canada. Amy's family tree shows you some of them. You and your partner must share information in order to complete the family tree.

A. Ask your partner these questions about Amy's family. Write the answers in the empty spaces in the family tree. Then, answer your partner's questions.

1. What is Amy's great-grandmother's name?
2. How old is Joe?
3. Who was Rosa married to?

4. What is Liz's half-brother's name?
5. What do you know about Amy's brother?

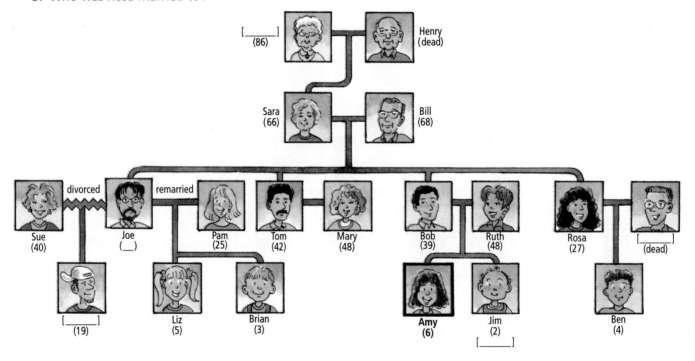

B. Discuss the answers to these questions about Amy's family tree with your partner. Write the answers below.

1. Who are the single (unmarried) mothers? _____
2. Who is married to a much younger woman? _____
3. Which couple has an adopted child? _____
4. Which couple doesn't have any children? _____
5. Who is divorced? _____

 Ask your partner these questions:
1. Do you have a large or small family?
2. Who is the oldest person in your family? The youngest?
3. Is divorce common in your country?

Breaking the News

EPISODE **5**

THEMES
- **Buying a Used Car**
- **A Shopping Mall**
- **Formal and Informal Clothes**

GAME
- **A Parent's Approval**

OPTIONAL PROJECT
- **Shopping for Clothes / (Appendix 5)**

THEME **Buying a Used Car**

 TEAM | **GAME** | Time: 10 min.

team number

In this episode, Rebecca looks for a used car. Match the photos of used cars with the advertisements below. The first team with the correct answers wins.

A great car for big families! **$3,750**	**STILL RUNS!** Cheap! **$600**	A classic car from the past. In good shape! **$10,000**
1. _____	2. _____	3. _____
Safe pick-up truck. Great for hauling things! **$8,500**	A great car for summer! Stay cool! **$5,799**	Sporty and fast! Rebuilt engine. **$7,000**
4. _____	5. _____	6. _____

group number

Your group is buying a used car to take on a long trip. You only have $4,000 to spend.

A. Talk with the people in your group. Decide which options to buy for the car. Look at the list below. If you don't understand the meaning of an item, ask your teacher. (**Note: you *must* choose one of the engines. Everything else is optional.)

B. Write your options and the costs in the spaces. Add up the total cost. Make sure your group doesn't spend more than $4,000.

Option	Cost
	$
	$
	$
	$
	$
	$
	$
	$
	$
	$
	$
TOTAL COST	$

OPTIONS	
Engine with 90,000 miles**	$ 1,250
Engine with 45,000 miles**	$ 2,950
Radio	$ 50
Radio with cassette player	$ 100
Power windows and door locks	$ 250
New tires	$ 400
New brakes	$ 400
Airbags	$ 1,250
Sunroof	$ 350
Car phone	$ 300
Four-wheel drive	$ 1,300
Leather seats	$ 2,000
Air conditioning	$ 2,000
New paint job	$ 1,500
1-year warranty	$ 700

THEME **A Shopping Mall**

partner's name

Do you like to go to shopping malls? Look at the types of stores in the list.

A. Write three stores you would go to, and one store you wouldn't go to.

B. Ask your partner these questions:
- *Which stores would you go to?*
- *Which store wouldn't you go to?*

C. Write your partner's answers.

- a shoe store
- an ice-cream parlor
- a department store
- a jewelry store
- a book store
- an electronics store
- a sports equipment/ clothing store
- a fast-food restaurant

Stores you would go to

1. _____
2. _____
3. _____

A store you wouldn't go to

_____

Stores your partner would go to

1. _____
2. _____
3. _____

A store your partner wouldn't go to

_____

THEME **Formal and Informal Clothes**

 4 GROUP **BRAINSTORM**

group number

In this episode, Rebecca goes shopping for some new clothes. She wants to buy some formal things to wear to special events. With your group, make a list of the *formal* and *informal* clothes that Rebecca might see as she shops. Use the words below, and add any others of your own.

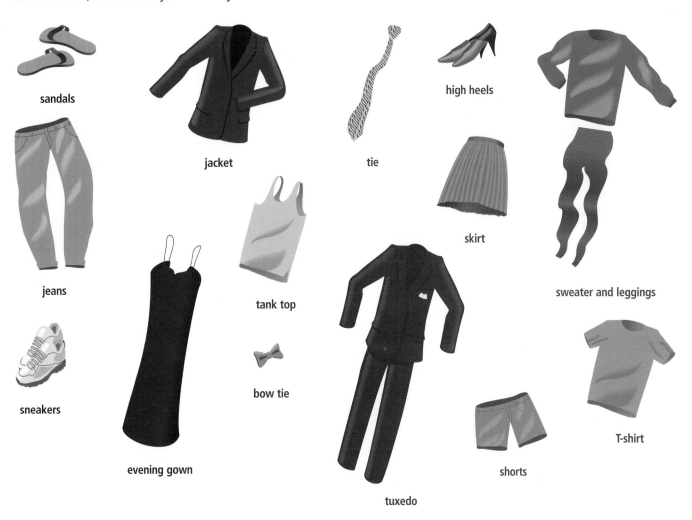

sandals

jacket

tie

high heels

jeans

tank top

skirt

sweater and leggings

sneakers

bow tie

evening gown

tuxedo

shorts

T-shirt

Formal clothes

Informal clothes

EPISODE **5** PAGE **3**

With your partner, act out a few conversations between a clothing salesperson and someone who is buying clothes for a special event.

A. Choose a special event from this box.

| a wedding | a job interview | a trip to _____ | a party | a special date |

B. Use the boxes below for help with your conversations. Remember to talk about the details of the event.

Details:	**When is it?**	**What kind is it?**	**Where is it?**	**What would you like?**
EXAMPLES	Salesperson: When's <u>your trip</u>? or What time is <u>the party</u>?	Customer: It's a <u>camping trip</u>. or It's a <u>formal party</u>.	Customer: The <u>interview</u> is <u>at a bank</u>. or The <u>wedding</u> is <u>outside in a garden</u>.	Customer: I want something <u>black</u>. or Salesperson: How about something <u>red</u>?

 What About YOU?

1. Are you more comfortable in formal or informal clothes?
2. What is your favorite item of clothing?
3. What kind of clothing do you wear to work?

GAME A Parent's Approval

Mr. Casey wants his children to be happy. However, parents don't always approve of the things that their children want. Play this game and decide how Mr. Casey would feel about Kevin and Rebecca's plans.

Get Ready to Play

Step One

Work by yourself. Cut a piece of paper in half. On one half, write two things that Kevin wants to do. On the other half, write two things that Rebecca wants to do. Use your imagination! Give both of your papers to your teacher. Don't tell anyone what you wrote!

EXAMPLE

Kevin

I want to get a job
after high shool.

I want to live in
my own apartment.

Rebecca

I want to go to
music school.

I want to drive to
San Francisco.

Step Two

Divide into teams of at least four people. Next, divide each team into two groups. Now you are ready to play.

Play the Game

■ Listen to your teacher read 15 sentences about Kevin and Rebecca. With your group, discuss how Mr. Casey would feel about each thing that Kevin and Rebecca want to do. Would he approve or disapprove? Check (✔) your answers without showing the other half of your team.

EXAMPLE   Your teacher reads: Statement 1. Kevin says, "I want to live in my own apartment."

Talk with the people in your group and check (✔) what Mr. Casey would do.

Statement	Approve	Disapprove	Point
1		✔	

You think Mr. Casey doesn't want Kevin to live in his own apartment.

■ When you've finished, join the other half of your team. Compare your answers to the 15 statements that your teacher read. Give your team a point for each answer that is the same. A total of 15 points is possible. The team with the most points wins. Use 15 different statements and play again!

Game Rules
■ Don't talk or listen to the other half of your team while you're working.
■ Don't change any answers after you've compared them with the other half of your team.

Does Mr. Casey approve or disapprove? Listen to your teacher, talk with your group, and check your answer. Then, compare your answers with those of the other half of your team. Give your team a point if your answer is the same.

Statement	Approve	Disapprove	Point
1			
2			
3			
4			
5			
6			
7			
8			
9			
10			
11			
12			
13			
14			
15			

TOTAL POINTS FOR OUR TEAM:

Saying Goodbye

EPISODE **6**

THEMES
- Saying Goodbye to Friends
- Music Lessons
- Junk Food

INFORMATION GAP
- Baseball

OPTIONAL PROJECT
- The Boston Red Sox (Appendix 6)

THEME Saying Goodbye to Friends

 1 | **PARTNER** | **WAYS TO SAY IT**

_____
partner's name

In this episode, Rebecca says goodbye to her friends on the softball team. Here are some expressions that people use when they won't see someone for a long time:

A	B
To show someone how you feel:	**To reply:**
I'm going to miss you.	I'm going to miss you, too.
I'll be thinking of you.	I'll be thinking of you, too.
To wish someone well:	**To reply:**
Take good care of yourself.	I will. Thank you.
Good (Best of) luck to you.	Thanks. Good luck to you, too.
To ask someone to communicate:	**To reply:**
Please stay (keep) in touch.	I will. And you do the same.
Don't forget to write (call).	I won't. Don't worry.

Work with a partner. Look at the situations below. One partner says goodbye with an expression from Column A above. The other partner replies with an expression from Column B above. Take turns. Then, make up your own situation.

EXAMPLE   Your co-worker gets a job in a different city.
            Student A: Best of luck to you.   Student B: Thanks. Good luck to you, too.

1. Your friend is moving far away.

Student A _____

Student B _____

2. Your brother/sister is joining the army.

Student A _____

Student B _____

3. Your teacher is retiring.

Student A _____

Student B _____

4. Your situation: _____

Student A _____

Student B _____

group number

Rebecca's friends give her a good-bye present and a card. The message inside the card says:

You're in our hearts, as you well know. We'll think of you, wherever you go. You'll be a hit in San Francisco!

A. Make a good-bye card. Fold a piece of paper in half. Draw a picture on the front.

B. Inside, write a message. You can use some expressions from Activity 1 or others of your own.

C. When you finish, share your card with the class. Vote on the best card.

THEME **Music Lessons**

3 TEAM **GAME** Time: 10 min.

team number

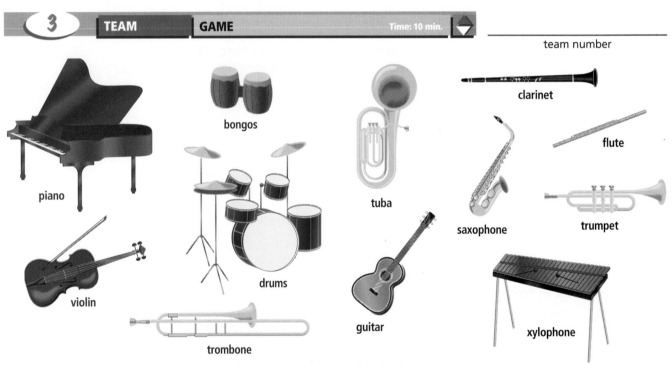

piano

bongos

clarinet

flute

tuba

saxophone

trumpet

violin

drums

guitar

xylophone

trombone

Look at the pictures above. Write the name of each musical instrument in the correct category below. Add instruments from your country, and any others that aren't on the list. The team with the most correct answers wins.

	Percussion	Woodwind	Brass	String
EXAMPLES	bongos	clarinet	tuba	piano

4 **CLASS** | **SURVEY**

Interview the people in your class.

A. Talk to as many people as you can. Ask these questions, and fill in the chart below.
- *Did you ever take music lessons?*
- *What instrument did you play?*
- *How many years did you take lessons?*
- *Are you still playing an instrument now?*

	Name	Instrument	Number of years	Still playing now?
EXAMPLE	Louie	clarinet	10	yes
1.				
2.				
3.				
4.				
5.				
6.				
7.				
8.				
9.				
10.				
11.				
12.				
13.				
14.				
15.				

B. As a class, discuss your charts. Answer these questions:
- *Which instrument(s) can most people play?* _____
- *Who studied for the longest time?* _____
- *How many people are still playing?* _____
- *Who can play the most instruments?*

1. What is your favorite musical instrument?
2. Why do you like this instrument?
3. Who is your favorite musician on this instrument?
4. What is your favorite song that uses this instrument?

THEME Junk Food

Sandy and Kevin eat potato chips at the softball game. Kevin likes to eat cookies and peanut butter together. These foods are "junk food." **Junk food** is full of sugar, fat, or salt and has few vitamins. **Fast food** is convenient, but it's usually high in fat, sugar, and salt. **Healthy food** is high in vitamins and low in fat, sugar, and salt.

A. Look at the following list of foods. Write the foods in the correct categories. Use your own paper.

B. Add more items to the categories. You can add foods from your country.

C. Make up a new category of food and add as many items as you can.

D. Compare your lists with another group. Discuss any answers that are different.

FOOD CATEGORIES

Healthy food   Junk food

Fast food   (Your category)

Has your diet changed? Do you eat the same foods as you used to eat? Ask your partner about his/her eating habits.

A. Ask what your partner eats _now_. Write the answers below. Ask this question: _What do you usually eat for _lunch_?_

breakfast _____

lunch _____

dinner _____

snack _____

B. Ask what your partner _used to_ eat. Write the answers below. Ask this question: _What did you used to eat for _lunch_?_

breakfast _____

lunch _____

dinner _____

snack _____

C. Compare the answers in A and B. Discuss the answers to these questions with your partner:
- _Is your partner's diet healthier now? Why?_
- _What can a person do to make his/her diet healthier?_

INFORMATION GAP **Baseball**

STUDENT A Work with a partner. One of you works on this page. The other works on page 6. Don't look at your partner's page.

Baseball is a very popular sport in the United States and Canada. Rebecca plays softball—a game very similar to baseball—with a group of her friends. In order to learn more about baseball, you and your partner need to share information. Each of you knows something different. Follow the directions in each part.

Part One

Read this paragraph about baseball. Answer your partner's questions.
Baseball is played on a field. A baseball field has two main parts: the infield and the outfield. Four bases are located in the infield. These bases are home plate, first, second, and third base. The pitcher's mound is also located in the infield. The pitcher's mound is a small dirt hill in the center of the infield. The pitcher stands on this mound and throws the baseball to the catcher. The catcher plays behind home plate.

Part Two

Ask these questions about your partner's paragraph.
Write your partner's answers.

1. How many players are on a baseball team?

2. How many players play in the outfield?

3. How many players play in the infield?

4. Which players are in the outfield?

5. Which players are in the infield?

6. Where does the shortstop play?

7. Where does the batter stand?

8. What does the batter try to do?

Part Three

In baseball, each time the batter misses the ball, it's called a **strike**. After the third strike, the batter's turn is over. Play this guessing game with your partner and try not to strike out.

■ Think of a baseball word from Parts One and Two. Give your partner a clue to help him/her guess the word.

■ Your partner has three chances to guess the word. Each incorrect guess is a strike. If your partner strikes out, it's your turn to guess.

EXAMPLE	
Partner A:	This person plays between two bases.
Partner B:	Is it the pitcher?
Partner A:	No. Strike one.
Partner B:	Is it the shortstop?
Partner A:	Yes, that's it.

Ask your partner these questions:
1. What is your favorite sport?
2. Do you like to play this sport, or do you like to watch it?
3. Who is your favorite athlete? What sport does he/she play?

INFORMATION GAP **Baseball**

| **1** | **PARTNER** | **INFORMATION GAP** | |

STUDENT **B** — Work with a partner. One of you works on this page. The other works on page 5. Don't look at your partner's page.

Baseball is a very popular sport in the United States and Canada. Rebecca plays softball—a game very similar to baseball—with a group of her friends. In order to learn more about baseball, you and your partner need to share information. Each of you knows something different. Follow the directions in each part.

Part One

Ask these questions about your partner's paragraph.
Write your partner's answers.

1. Where do you play baseball?

2. What are the two main parts of the field called?

3. How many bases are there?

4. What are the names of these bases?

5. In what part of the field are these bases located?

6. Where is the pitcher's mound located?

7. What does a pitcher do?

8. Where does a catcher play?

Part Two

Read this paragraph about baseball. Answer your partner's questions.
There are nine players on a baseball team. Three players play in the outfield. These players are the left fielder, center fielder, and right fielder. Six players play in the infield. These players are the pitcher, catcher, first baseman, second baseman, shortstop, and third baseman. The shortstop plays between the second baseman and third baseman. The batter stands next to home plate and tries to hit the baseball when the pitcher throws it.

Part Three

In baseball, each time the batter misses the ball, it's called a **strike**. After the third strike, the batter's turn is over. Play this guessing game with your partner and try not to strike out.

- Think of a baseball word from Parts One and Two. Give your partner a clue to help him/her guess the word.

- Your partner has three chances to guess the word. Each incorrect guess is a strike. If your partner strikes out, it's your turn to guess.

EXAMPLE	
Partner A:	This person plays between two bases.
Partner B:	Is it the pitcher?
Partner A:	No. Strike one.
Partner B:	Is it the shortstop?
Partner A:	Yes, that's it.

Ask your partner these questions:
1. What is your favorite sport?
2. Do you like to play this sport, or do you like to watch it?
3. Who is your favorite athlete? What sport does he/she play?

Leaving Home

EPISODE **7**

THEMES
- Surprises
- Presents
- Good Luck / Bad Luck

GAME
- A Trip Across the U.S. with Rebecca

OPTIONAL PROJECT
- Discovering the United States (Appendix 7)

THEME **Surprises**

| **1** | **PARTNER** | **WAYS TO SAY IT** | |

_____
partner's name

I can't believe it.

In this episode, Rebecca was surprised when her father gave her a car. Here are some ways that people show they are surprised in English:

You're kidding (joking).	Really? Wow! That's great!	I'm speechless.	What a surprise!
You must be kidding (joking).	I can't (don't) believe it!	I don't know what to say!	Get out of here!

Work with a partner. Look at the situations below. Take turns. One person chooses a situation. The other person chooses an expression to show surprise. Then, make up your own situations.

EXAMPLE   Student A: I got an "A" on my English test.   Student B: Really? That's great!

Situations

1. I won the lottery.

2. My best friend is getting married.

3. My brother (sister, friend, and so on) is coming to visit.

4. Your situation:

Expressions

_____

_____

_____

_____

What About YOU?

1. Have you ever been surprised?
2. If so, what was the surprise?
3. Do you prefer to give or get surprises?

motorcycle

in-line skates

video

tickets

hat

leather jacket

shirts

cassette

necklace

ring

sneakers

CD

bracelet

earrings

skateboard

bicycle

Look at the presents in the picture. Circle five presents you like, and write them below. Ask your partner this question: *What presents do you like?* Write your partner's answers.

Presents you like

1. _____
2. _____
3. _____
4. _____
5. _____

Presents your partner likes

1. _____
2. _____
3. _____
4. _____
5. _____

A. Look at the picture in Activity 2. Write the name of each present in the correct category below.

B. Add one more present for each category.

C. Make up a new category with five presents. The team with the most correct answers wins.

Jewelry

1. bracelet
2. _____
3. _____
4. _____
5. _____

Clothing

1. sneakers
2. _____
3. _____
4. _____
5. _____

Things with wheels

1. bicycle
2. _____
3. _____
4. _____
5. _____

Entertainment

1. cassette
2. _____
3. _____
4. _____
5. _____

Other category

1. _____
2. _____
3. _____
4. _____
5. _____

4 | **PARTNER** | **ROLE-PLAY**

partner's name

Do this role-play with your partner. One of you will pretend to shop for three people. The other person will pretend to be a salesperson at the store. The salesperson will tell the shopper what to buy. If you are the shopper, describe the people you are buying presents for to the salesperson. What do they like? If you are the salesperson, describe the items in your store. Why would someone want to buy them?

People on your shopping list

1. _____
2. _____
3. _____

Presents your partner suggests

1. _____
2. _____
3. _____

THEME **Good Luck/Bad Luck**

In the United States and Canada, a four-leaf clover is a sign of good luck. A broken mirror is a sign of bad luck. Divide into groups. Write the names of three signs of good luck and three signs of bad luck in your country. Discuss your answers with your group.

	Good luck	Bad luck
EXAMPLE	four-leaf clover	a broken mirror
1.		
2.		
3.		
Most unusual answer		

In the United States, people who believe in good or bad luck are called **superstitious**. Divide into groups. Find out how many people in your group are superstitious. Ask this question: *Are you superstitious?*

Name	Sex	When is your birthday?			Are you superstitious?		
	(M/F)	January –April	May –August	September –December	Very	A little	Not at all
1.							
2.							
3.							
4.							
5.							
6.							

Look at the opinion survey in Activity 6. Compare surveys with a partner from a different group. Answer these questions.

1. Who are more superstitious, men or women?

   Number of superstitious men: _____   Number of superstitious women: _____

2. Which birthday months have the most superstitious people? _____

3. Which birthday months have the fewest superstitious people? _____

GAME **A Trip Across the U.S. with Rebecca**

 | **TEAM** | **GAME** | ⬍ | _____

In this episode, Rebecca is going to leave Boston and drive to San Francisco. Play this game, and cross the United States with Rebecca. The team that gets to California first wins.

Get Ready to Play

Step One

Divide into four teams. Each team writes 20 questions and answers about the story so far. Work with your team to write five questions and answers for each of the categories below. Use your own paper.

	Who?	**What?**	**Where?**	**Why?**
EXAMPLE	Who plays the guitar? (Rebecca)	What is the name of Rebecca's brother? (Kevin)	Where is Rebecca going to college? (San Francisco)	Why does Rebecca leave home? (She wants to go to college.)
	1.	1.	1.	1.
	2.	2.	2.	2.
	3.	3.	3.	3.
	4.	4.	4.	4.
	5.	5.	5.	5.

Step Two

After your teacher checks your team's questions and answers, copy the questions on separate pieces of paper (or index cards). Write the questions and your team's number on the front. Write the answers on the back.

Step Three

Cut out the die and the other game pieces on Appendix 13. Each team should pick one car and one game marker.

FRONT

BACK

Play the Game

- Each team puts its square marker on the gameboard at **GO** and its car in the state of Massachusetts.
- One player from each team arranges the question cards in four piles—who, what, where, and why. This player will ask the questions for the team seated across from him/her.
- Decide who goes first. Roll the die. The team with the highest number starts, and play continues to the right.
- The first team rolls the die, and moves its marker the number of spaces indicated (if a 2 is rolled, the marker is moved two spaces, and so on).
- If a team lands on a question space (who, what, where, or why), that team member must answer a question from that card pile to move on.
- If the team's answer is correct, the team member is allowed to move the car one state closer to California. He/she gets to roll the die again, and take another turn. If the team's answer is incorrect, that team loses its turn. Play continues to the right with the next team.
- If the team lands on a **DETOUR** space, the team member must move the car to the state that is indicated and lose a turn. On the next turn, he/she will start from that state on his/her way to California.
- The first team to get its car to California wins.

GAME A Trip Across the U.S. with Rebecca

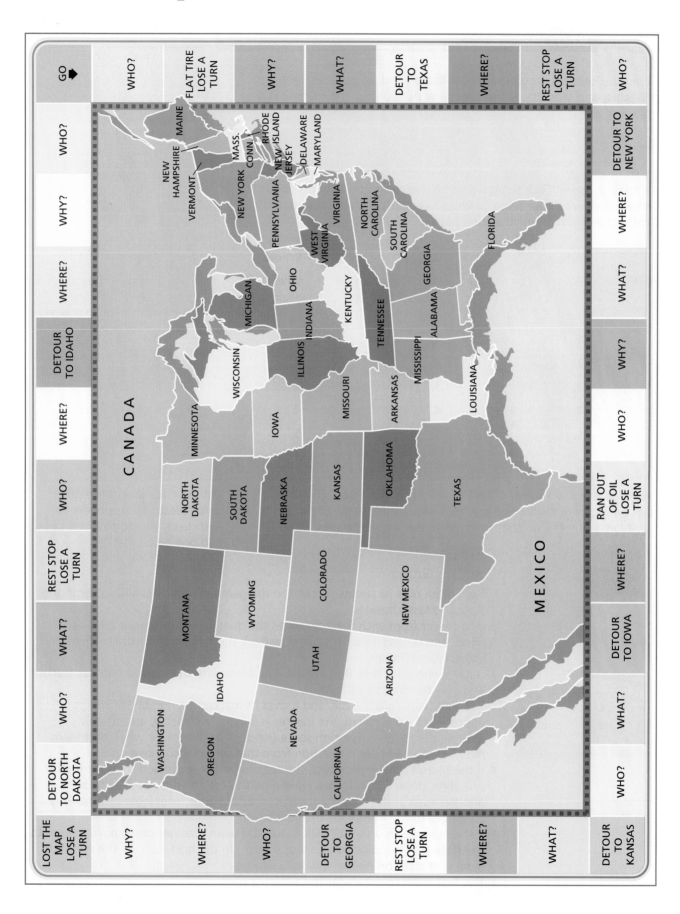

The Stranger

EPISODE **8**

THEMES
- Talking to Strangers
- Being Afraid
- Car Trouble

SONG
- Where's My Baby?

OPTIONAL PROJECT
- The Desert
  (Appendix 8)

THEME Talking to Strangers

1 | **PARTNER** | **INTERVIEW**

partner's name

1

2

3

4

5

A. Look at the five pictures above. Pretend you are the person in each picture. Would you talk to the stranger? Check (✔) your answers below.

B. Ask your partner this question: *Would you talk to the stranger in picture* __1__ *?* Check (✔) your partner's answers.

You		Picture	Your partner	
Yes	No		Yes	No
		1		
		2		
		3		
		4		
		5		

In this episode, Rebecca meets a stranger named Alberto. When her car breaks down in the desert, she goes with Alberto to look for a phone. Is this a good decision? Should Rebecca trust this stranger?

A. Divide into two groups. If you agree with Opinion 1 below, join group 1. If you agree with Opinion 2, join group 2.

B. With your group, make a list of reasons to support your opinion. Be ready to explain each one.

C. Take turns. Each group has five minutes to present its ideas.

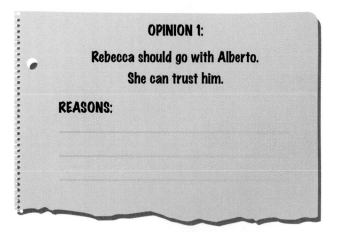

OPINION 1:

Rebecca should go with Alberto.
She can trust him.

REASONS:

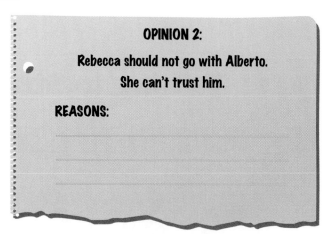

OPINION 2:

Rebecca should not go with Alberto.
She can't trust him.

REASONS:

What About YOU?

1. Should a child ever speak to strangers?
2. Did your parents give you advice about talking to strangers?
3. Have you ever felt uncomfortable when a stranger spoke to you?

THEME **Being Afraid**

On a piece of paper, write something that you're afraid of. Don't show your paper to anyone else. If you're not afraid of anything, write, "I'm not afraid of anything." Here are some examples:

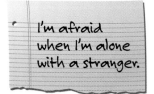

I'm afraid when I'm alone with a stranger.

I'm afraid to fly.

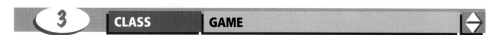

I'm afraid of insects.

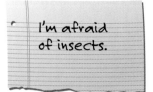

I'm always afraid when I get lost.

Give your paper to the teacher. The teacher will read each paper out loud. Try to guess which person wrote the sentence. If the class hasn't made the correct guess after three tries, the person who wrote the sentence must stand up and identify him or herself.

_____
partner's name

A phobia is a very strong fear of something. Work with a partner to match the phobias with the situations below. Write the number of the phobia next to the correct situation.

Phobias	Definitions
1. acrophobia	fear of high places
2. agoraphobia	fear of public places
3. astraphobia	fear of thunder and lightning
4. claustrophobia	fear of enclosed places
5. hemophobia	fear of blood
6. hydrophobia	fear of water
7. nyctophobia	fear of night
8. photophobia	fear of light
9. xenophobia	fear of strangers
10. zoophobia	fear of animals

Situations

_____ **A.** You don't like being in cars, elevators, or telephone booths.

_____ **B.** You never want to go swimming, water skiing, or scuba diving.

_____ **C.** You don't have a family pet such as a dog or a cat.

_____ **D.** You close the curtains and don't let the sun inside.

_____ **E.** You don't want to meet new people or make new friends.

Situations

_____ **F.** You don't like to watch medical programs on television.

_____ **G.** You don't like to go to the shopping mall or any other places filled with people.

_____ **H.** You hide under the bed when a rainstorm begins.

_____ **I.** You don't like climbing mountains or flying in airplanes.

_____ **J.** You turn on all of the lights and don't want to go to sleep.

5 **GROUP** **GAME**

_____
group number

Work in a group. Make up some of your own phobias. Be creative! For example, "bookophobia" could be "fear of reading." When you finish, have someone in the group read them out loud to the class. Can anyone guess your phobias? Vote on the funniest phobia.

	Phobias	**Definitions**
EXAMPLE	bookophobia	fear of reading

THEME Car Trouble

Have you ever had car trouble? Look at the three situations below. Circle the things you would do in each situation. Compare your answers with those of a partner. Did you choose the same things? Explain the reasons for your answers.

Situation 1

I <u>would/wouldn't</u> be nervous.
I would <u>stay with/leave</u> the car.
I would try to <u>fix the car/get help</u>.
I <u>would/wouldn't</u> call a mechanic.

Situation 2

I <u>would/wouldn't</u> be nervous.
I would <u>stay with/leave</u> the car.
I would try to <u>fix the car/get help</u>.
I <u>would/wouldn't</u> call a mechanic.

Situation 3

*Oh, no!
Out of gas!*

I <u>would/wouldn't</u> be nervous.
I would <u>stay with/leave the car</u>.
I would try to <u>fix the car/get help</u>.
I <u>would/wouldn't</u> call a mechanic.

SONG **Where's My Baby?**

As Rebecca drives across the desert, she listens to some **Tex-Mex** music on the radio. She says it sounds different from the music she hears in Boston. **Tex-Mex** or **Tejano** music is a combination of Texan and Mexican musical styles. It is very popular in the southwestern part of the United States.

With a partner, read the words to the Tex-Mex song that Rebecca hears on the radio. Answer the questions together.

> Where's My Baby?
>
> 1 She's not the kind to stay in one place for too long,
> 2 you don't have to tell me that.
> 3 She's not the kind whose love will be true and strong,
> 4 you don't have to tell me that.
>
> 5 Don't tell me her eyes are bright,
> 6 and she loves to dance 'til the morning light.
> 7 All I want to know is,
> 8 where's my baby tonight?
>
> 9 So, where's my baby? Can anybody say?
> 10 One day she's here beside me, the next day she's in L.A.
> 11 Yeah, where's my baby? What's this all about?
> 12 One day, she's here, the next she's moving out.
>
> 13 Yeah, where's my baby? Does anybody know?
> 14 One day she's down in Memphis, the next day in Mexico.
> 15 So, where's my baby? Where's my baby gone?
> 16 One day she's here, the next she's moving on.

1. Who is singing this song? A man or a woman?

2. Read lines 1-4. What is the singer saying about "my baby"?

3. Write the names of the places where the singer's "baby" goes.

4. Is the singer sad or happy? Tell why.

What is the singer like? What is "my baby" like? Describe them. Then, compare your ideas with your partner's ideas.

You	Your partner
The singer is. . .	The singer is. . .
"My baby" is. . .	"My baby" is. . .

SONG **Where's My Baby?**

Do you like to sing along with songs on the radio? Do you ever make up your own words to popular songs?

A. Work with your group to change the words to "Where's My Baby?"
Your song can be about anything.

B. Choose one person to sing or read the new song to the rest of the class.

> Where's My _____?
>
> 1   _____,
>
> 2   you don't have to tell me that.
>
> 3   _____,
>
> 4   you don't have to tell me that.
>
> 5   Don't tell me _____,
>
> 6   and _____.
>
> 7   All I want to know is,
>
> 8   where's my _____?
>
> 9   So, where's my _____? Can anybody say?
>
> 10   One day _____, the next day _____.
>
> 11   Yeah, where's my _____? What's this all about?
>
> 12   One day, _____.
>
> 13   Yeah, where's my _____? Does anybody know?
>
> 14   One day _____.
>
> 15   So, where's my _____? Where's my _____ gone?
>
> 16   One day _____.

What About YOU?

1. Do you ever listen to the radio? What station do you like to listen to?
2. Does the area where you live have a special kind of music?
3. Do you know all the words to any song? Which one?

The Motel

EPISODE **9**

THEMES
- Being Polite
- Helping Someone
- Answering Machines

INFORMATION GAP
- Dating

OPTIONAL PROJECT
- Staying in a Motel
  (Appendix 9)

THEME **Being Polite**

 1 | **PARTNER** | **DISCUSSION** ▲ _____

partner's name

the restaurant worker ____

the motel clerk ____

Rebecca ____   Alberto ____

Alberto ____   the truck driver ____

With your partner, discuss what's happening in the pictures above.

A. Decide how polite each person is. Use the scale provided.

B. Write your answers in the spaces after each person's name.

C. Compare your answers with those of another pair. Do you have different opinions? Discuss the reasons for your answers.

1 = very polite

2 = polite

3 = not polite/not rude

4 = a little rude

5 = rude

_____
partner's name

In this episode, Rebecca and Alberto try to make polite requests. Here are some ways to make polite requests in English:

May I leave class early today?	**Could I** ask you a question?	**Would you mind** waiting?
Would it be possible to use your phone?	**Could you** pass the salt, please?	**Can I** please borrow your pen?

Work with a partner. Look at the situations below. Take turns. One person chooses a situation. The other person makes a polite request using one of the expressions above. Then, make up your own situation.

Situations

Expressions

EXAMPLE   You want to see a friend's notes from class.   Would you mind showing me your notes?

1. Your neighbor's music is too loud. _____

2. You want your teacher to repeat something. _____

3. You need to borrow two eggs from your neighbor. _____

4. Your situation: _____

1. Are you always polite?
2. Were you ever too angry to be polite?
3. Has anyone been rude to you lately? If so, how did you respond?

THEME **Helping Someone**

3 | **GROUP** | **BRAINSTORM**

_____
group number

Alberto helps Rebecca many times in this episode. In groups, list all the helpful things Alberto does for Rebecca. When you're finished, compare answers with the rest of the class. Which group thought of the most things?

1. _____
2. _____
3. _____
4. _____
5. _____
6. _____
7. _____
8. _____
9. _____
10. _____

4   **CLASS**   **GAME**

A. Think of a problem that requires help from someone else. Write this problem on a piece of paper. Don't let anyone see your paper.

EXAMPLES

My car broke down.

I left my money at home.

I missed the bus.

B. Stand up and get in a circle. Tape your paper onto the back of the student who is standing in front of you.

C. Walk around the room. Look at people's backs. Offer them help. Other students will offer you help. Try to guess what your problem is.

D. When you have guessed your problem, sit down. See how long it takes your class to guess all of the problems.

1. Do you always offer help when people need it?
2. Does someone always offer help when you need it?
3. How do you feel about asking for help?

THEME **Answering Machines**

5   **GROUP**   **SURVEY**

group number

In this episode, Rebecca calls the mechanic and leaves a message on his answering machine. How do you feel about answering machines?

A. Read the questions in the chart below, and check (✔) *Yes* or *No*.

B. Ask two other group members the questions. Write their answers in the chart.

	You		Group member 1		Group member 2	
	Yes	No	Yes	No	Yes	No
1. Do you have an answering machine?	❑	❑	❑	❑	❑	❑
2. Do you like to talk to an answering machine?	❑	❑	❑	❑	❑	❑
3. Do you leave messages on answering machines?	❑	❑	❑	❑	❑	❑
4. Are you ever glad to get an answering machine?	❑	❑	❑	❑	❑	❑

1   **2**

In the United States and Canada, many people talk to an answering machine everyday. Look at pictures 1 and 2 and then complete the activities below.

A. With your partner, write two messages like Steve's (picture 1) to put on your answering machine. Be creative! Read your messages to the class and vote on the best ones.

B. Role-play with your partner. You pretend to call your partner, but he/she is not home. Your partner pretends to be an answering machine, like in picture 1. You leave a message, like in picture 2. Then switch roles.

INFORMATION GAP **Dating**

STUDENT A Work with a partner. One of you works on this page. The other works on page 6. Don't look at your partner's page.

People who have things in common often date each other. Rebecca and Alberto are both artists. He's a photographer, she's a musician. Do you think they will begin to date?

Look at the people below. Your partner has different people on his/her page. Talk with your partner and try to decide which person on your page would probably date another person on your partner's page.

Part One

A. Describe these six people to your partner. Tell as much as you can about what they look like, what they are wearing, what they are doing, and where they are. Answer your partner's questions.

B. Listen as your partner describes the people on his/her page. Ask your partner questions.

C. Without looking at your partner's page, talk about which people should date each other. Decide on your answers together and write them underneath the pictures.

Brooke

Thomas

David

Beth

Hillary

Eric

Brooke should date _____   Thomas should date _____

David should date _____   Beth should date _____

Hillary should date _____   Eric should date _____

Part Two

A. Look at the people on your partner's page. Did you do a good job of deciding which people should date each other? Now that you can see the people on your partner's page, would you change any couples?

B. Compare answers with the rest of the class. Did most people have the same answers? What are some of the most unusual couples?

INFORMATION GAP **Dating**

STUDENT B Work with a partner. One of you works on this page. The other works on page 5. Don't look at your partner's page.

People who have things in common often date each other. Rebecca and Alberto are both artists. He's a photographer, she's a musician. Do you think they will begin to date?

Look at the people below. Your partner has different people on his/her page. Talk with your partner and try to decide which person on your page would probably date another person on your partner's page.

Part One

A. Describe these six people to your partner. Tell as much as you can about what they look like, what they are wearing, what they are doing, and where they are. Answer your partner's questions.

B. Listen as your partner describes the people on his/her page. Ask your partner questions.

C. Without looking at your partner's page, talk about which people should date each other. Decide on your answers together and write them underneath the pictures.

Cecilia

André

Jimmy

Laura

Bill

Debby

Cecilia should date _____   André should date _____

Jimmy should date _____   Laura should date _____

Bill should date _____   Debby should date _____

Part Two

A. Look at the people on your partner's page. Did you do a good job of deciding which people should date each other? Now that you can see the people on your partner's page, would you change any couples?

B. Compare answers with the rest of the class. Did most people have the same answers? What are some of the most unusual couples?

Negotiations

EPISODE **10**

THEMES
- Good and Bad Dreams
- Bargaining
- Selling Your Car

GAME
- Car Repairs

OPTIONAL PROJECT
- Native Americans (Appendix 10)

T H E M E Good and Bad Dreams

1 GROUP SURVEY ▲

group number

In this episode, Alberto and Rebecca talk about good and bad dreams. Bad dreams are also called **nightmares.** How many people in your group have had the good dreams and the nightmares in the pictures below? Write the number of people next to each dream.

Good dreams

a. You're flying. _____

b. You're swimming under water. _____

c. You're speaking English. _____

Nightmares

d. You're falling. _____

e. Someone is chasing you. _____

f. You're lost. _____

1. What's the most common good dream in your group? _____

2. What's the most common nightmare in your group? _____

3. Compare your answers with those of another group.
   Are the answers similar? _____

What About YOU?

1. Do you usually remember your dreams?
2. What was your favorite dream?
3. Do you ever have nightmares?
4. What was your worst nightmare?

2 TEAM GAME Time: 10 min.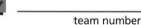

How many words can you make with the letters in the word NIGHTMARE?
- Divide into teams of two or three people.
- Use three or more letters in each word.
- Don't use any letter more than once in the same word. The team with the most words wins.

Nightmare

EXAMPLE right

_____ _____ _____

_____ _____ _____

_____ _____ _____

_____ _____ _____

_____ _____ _____

T H E M E **Bargaining**

3 GROUP DISCUSSION

In this episode, Rebecca bargains with Joe, the auto mechanic. They bargain over the price of her car. Divide into groups. Discuss bargaining in countries that your group members are from or have visited. In those countries, do people bargain in shops, outdoor markets, or taxis?

A. Check (✔) *Yes* or *No* for each question below. Give answers for as many countries as you can.

B. Compare your answers with those of another group. Are there different answers for the same country?

Country	Do people bargain in shops?		Do people bargain at outdoor markets?		Do people bargain in taxis?	
	Yes	No	Yes	No	Yes	No
	❑	❑	❑	❑	❑	❑
	❑	❑	❑	❑	❑	❑
	❑	❑	❑	❑	❑	❑
	❑	❑	❑	❑	❑	❑
	❑	❑	❑	❑	❑	❑
	❑	❑	❑	❑	❑	❑
	❑	❑	❑	❑	❑	❑
	❑	❑	❑	❑	❑	❑

 **What About YOU?**
1. Do you ever have the chance to bargain?
2. If yes, what do you like to bargain for?
3. If no, would you like to have the chance to bargain?

People in the United States often bargain at **tag sales**. Tag sales (also called **garage sales**) are common on weekends. People put used things outside their homes and try to sell them. You and your partner are at a tag sale. Look at the items for sale in the picture below.

A. Decide who will be the buyer and the seller.

B. The buyer tries to buy each item for a low price. The seller tries to sell each item for a high price.

C. Bargain for the price of *all of the items* in the picture.

D. Write the final price for each item in the chart below.

E. Add up the total cost of all of the items and write it in the space below.

F. Compare the results with the rest of the class.
  ■ *Which pair had the lowest total price for all the items?*
    That pair had the best buyer in the class.
  ■ *Which pair had the highest total price for all the items?*
    That pair had the best seller in the class.

Item	Final purchase price
1. desk lamp	$ _____
2. vase	$ _____
3. dictionary	$ _____
4. coffee mug	$ _____
5. bicycle	$ _____
Total	$ _____

THEME Selling Your Car

5 **PARTNER** **INTERVIEW**

Almost new
Honda Civic

10,000 miles

Excellent
condition

Pretend that you're selling this car in your country.

A. Answer the following questions about how you would sell the car and how much money you would ask for it. Check (✔) your answers.

B. Then, interview your partner. Check (✔) his/her answers.

C. Compare your answers. Discuss any answers that are different.

Would *you* try to sell the car. . .		Would *your partner* try to sell the car. . .	
in a newspaper ad?	❏	in a newspaper ad?	❏
by telling people about it?	❏	by telling people about it?	❏
in a magazine ad?	❏	in a magazine ad?	❏
on the Internet?	❏	on the Internet?	❏
to a dealer?	❏	to a dealer?	❏
to a friend?	❏	to a friend?	❏
other?	❏	other?	❏

How much money would you ask
for the car? _____

How much money would you accept
for the car? _____

How much money would your partner
ask for the car? _____

How much money would your partner
accept for the car? _____

1. Do you know someone who bought a used car?
2. Did he/she have any problems with it?
3. Is it a good idea to buy a used car?
4. Where would you buy a used car?

GAME **Car Repairs**

In this episode, Joe doesn't have all the parts he needs to fix Rebecca's car.

Speech bubble: *I don't have the right part. It'll take at least a day or two.*

Now Joe is trying to fix your car! In this game, the first player to get all the necessary car parts wins.

Get Ready to Play

Step One
Divide into groups of four players. One person in each group cuts out all the cards on Appendix 10. These are the game cards. Put the cards face down on a table and mix them up.

Step Two
Each player takes a different list of parts on page 6. These are the parts Joe needs to fix the car. The winner of the game is the first person to collect all of the cards that match the four car parts on his/her list.

Step Three
Each player picks four game cards. Now you are ready to play.

Play the Game
■ Decide who will go first.
■ Each player can ask one question at each turn. Ask any other player a question in order to get one of the game cards you need.

EXAMPLE

Player 1   Do you have a ____*muffler*____?
                                     (car part)

Player 2   Yes, I do. Here it is.
                 or
                 No, I don't. Sorry.

■ If the player has the game card you ask for, he/she must give it to you. If the player does not have the card you want, play continues to the right.
■ The first player to get all the parts on his/her list wins the game.

G A M E **Car Repairs**

Choose one of the lists below. Try to collect all of the game cards that match the parts on your list!

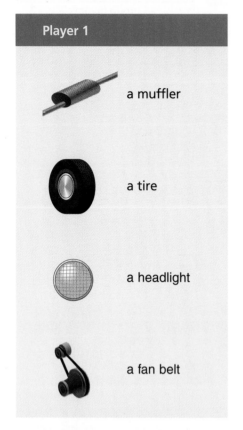

Player 1

a muffler

a tire

a headlight

a fan belt

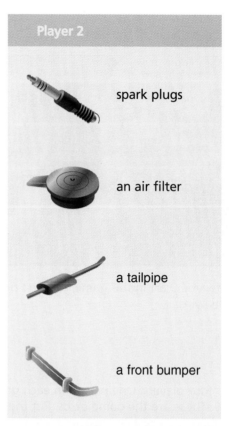

Player 2

spark plugs

an air filter

a tailpipe

a front bumper

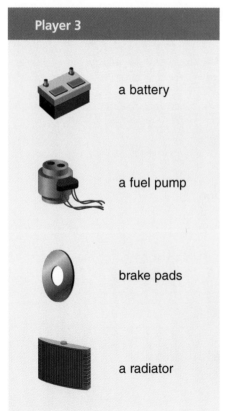

Player 3

a battery

a fuel pump

brake pads

a radiator

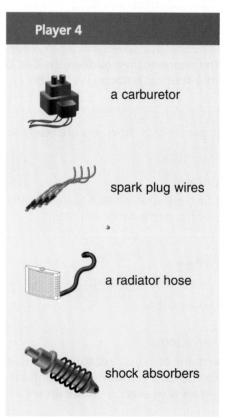

Player 4

a carburetor

spark plug wires

a radiator hose

shock absorbers

Photos and Farewells

EPISODE **11**

THEMES
■ Taking Photos
■ Taking a Bus Trip
■ Speeding

INFORMATION GAP
■ Immigrants in the U.S.

OPTIONAL PROJECT
■ Nature and Natural Beauty (Appendix 11)

THEME **Taking Photos**

1 **GROUP**   **DISCUSSION**

group number

Imagine that Alberto is visiting the place where you live. He asks for your advice about where to go to take pictures. What would you tell him?

A. Divide into groups. Agree on one answer for each question below. Write your group's suggestions on the lines.

Alberto asks	Your group's suggestion
"Where should I go to take pictures?"	
"What's the best season to take pictures there?"	
"What's the best time of day to go there?"	
"Where should I go to take pictures of people?"	

B. As a class, discuss each group's suggestions. Which answers were the most popular? Write them below.

What About YOU?

1. Do you like to take photographs?
2. Do you have photographs on your walls at home?
3. Have you ever gone somewhere just to take photographs?

In this episode, Alberto asks Rebecca if he can take a picture of her. Here are some ways that people make requests to take a picture:

Would you mind if I take a picture of you?	**Could you please** take a picture of me?	**Can I** use a flash in here?
May I take a picture of your beautiful garden?	**Is it all right to** take pictures in here?	**Say cheese!** Smile!

Work with a partner. Look at the situations below. Take turns. One person chooses a situation. The other person uses one of the expressions from above. Then, make up your own situations.

	Situations	**Expressions**
EXAMPLE	a beautiful old house	Would you mind if I take a picture of your house?

You want to take a picture of...

1. a painting in an art museum.   _____

2. a famous person.   _____

3. friends of yours, but they aren't smiling.   _____

4. Your situation: _____

5. Your partner's situation: _____

THEME **Taking a Bus Trip**

Have you ever taken a bus trip? Look at the list of some common things people do on a bus trip.

A. Circle three activities that you would do and write them below.

B. Ask your partner: _What things would you do on a bus trip?_ Write your partner's answers below.

C. Finally, with your partner, think of two more things that you can do on a bus trip.

read	write a letter	eat	talk to other people
listen to music	play cards	sleep	look at the scenery

Things you would do on a bus trip

1. _____

2. _____

3. _____

Things your partner would do on a bus trip

1. _____

2. _____

3. _____

Two other things someone can do on a bus trip

1. _____

2. _____

You're buying a bus ticket from Boston to another city. Your partner is the clerk at the ticket window. Role-play the situations below with your partner. Look at the bus schedule for information about destinations, prices, and departure times. Write the final price and time in the line after each situation. Take turns. Then, make up your own situations.

BUS SCHEDULE
Boston Terminal

Destination	Prices (one way)	Prices (round trip)	Departure times
Chicago	$115	$230	6 AM, 8:30, 11, 2 PM, 5, 9
Los Angeles	$165	$330	5:30 AM, 8, 12 PM, 3, 7
New York	$29	$58	5 AM, 7, 9, 11, 1 PM, 3, 5, 7, 9
San Francisco	$169	$338	6 AM, 11, 3:30 PM, 8
Seattle	$199	$398	8:30 AM, 6:30 PM
Washington, D.C.	$45	$90	6 AM, 8, 11, 1 PM, 3, 5, 7, 9

EXAMPLE

Situations	Price	Time
EXAMPLE a round trip ticket to San Francisco, leaving in the afternoon	$338	3:30

You would like to buy…

1. a one way ticket to New York, leaving in the morning. _____ _____

2. a one way ticket to Chicago, leaving in the afternoon. _____ _____

3. a round trip ticket to Seattle, leaving early in the morning. _____ _____

4. a round trip ticket to Washington, D.C., leaving late in the evening. _____ _____

5. a one way ticket to Los Angeles, leaving very early in the morning. _____ _____

6. Your situation: _____ _____

7. Your partner's situation: _____ _____

THEME **Speeding**

5	GROUP	SURVEY	<div align="right">▲▼</div>

group number

Across most of the United States, the speed limit for highway driving is
55 miles per hour.

A. Divide into groups. Ask these questions:
- *What is the speed limit in your country?*
- *Do you think the speed limit in your country is too low, too high,
  or just right?*

B. Write the responses below.

C. Work with one person from a different group. Compare surveys and answer
the questions below.

Name	**Sex (M/F)**	**Country and speed limit**	**How is the speed limit in your country? Check (✔) one.**		
			too low	too high	just right

1. How many people think the speed limit in their country is too low? _____ too high? _____ just right? _____

2. Is there a relationship between the sex of the person and his/her opinion
   about the speed limit? Fill in the blanks below.

   Number of women who said "too low" _____   Number of men who said "too low" _____

   Number of women who said "too high" _____   Number of men who said "too high" _____

   Number of women who said "just right" _____   Number of men who said "just right" _____

6	PARTNER	ROLE-PLAY	<div align="right">▲▼</div>

partner's name

Role-play a scene between
a police officer and a person
stopped for speeding (the
speeder). You may choose one
of the following scenarios, or
you may make up your own.
Each pair must present its
"skit" to the class.

1. The speeder asks the police officer not to give him/her a ticket by explaining
   what a bad day he/she has had.

2. The speeder tries to offer the police officer a bribe. (A bribe is money or a
   gift offered to influence another person.)

3. The speeder explains that he/she is late for something important—a wedding,
   for example.

4. The speeder acts surprised that he/she was speeding because his/her
   speedometer is broken.

8 | PARTNER | INFORMATION GAP

partner's name

STUDENT **A** Work with a partner. One of you works on this page. The other works on page 6. Don't look at your partner's page!

The United States is a country of immigrants. For example, in this episode you learned that Alberto's family came to the United States from Mexico. Rebecca's grandparents came from Ireland.

Each of the United States celebrities below (or his/her family) came from another country. Ask your partner questions to find out which country each person below is from. Use these models:

Q: Where was Arnold Schwarzenegger born?

A: He was born in Austria.

Q: Where is Kristi Yamaguchi's family from?

A: Her family is from Japan.

Linda Ronstadt
singer
Her family is from _____ .

Arnold Schwarzenegger
actor
Born in Austria.

Hakeem Olajuwon
basketball player
Born in _____ .

Gloria Estefan
singer
Born in Cuba.

Bruce Lee
actor / martial artist
His family is from _____ .

Martina Navratilova
tennis player
Born in _____ .

Albert Einstein
scientist
Born in Germany.

Kristi Yamaguchi
figure skater
Her family is from Japan.

Dan Aykroyd
actor/comedian/singer
Born in _____ .

Mikhail Baryshnikov
dancer
Born in Russia.

INFORMATION GAP **Immigrants in the U.S.**

8 **PARTNER** **INFORMATION GAP**

partner's name

STUDENT B Work with a partner. One of you works on this page. The other works on page 5. Don't look at your partner's page!

The United States is a country of immigrants. For example, in this episode you learned that Alberto's family came to the United States from Mexico. Rebecca's grandparents came from Ireland.

Each of the United States celebrities below (or his/her family) came from another country. Ask your partner questions to find out which country each person below is from. Use these models:

Q: Where was Dan Aykroyd born?

A: He was born in Canada.

Q: Where is Linda Ronstadt's family from?

A: Her family is from Mexico.

Linda Ronstadt
singer
Her family is from Mexico.

Arnold Schwarzenegger
actor
Born in _____.

Bruce Lee
actor / martial artist
His family is from China.

Hakeem Olajuwon
basketball player
Born in Nigeria.

Gloria Estefan
singer
Born in _____.

Martina Navratilova
tennis player
Born in Czechoslovakia.

Albert Einstein
scientist
Born in _____.

Kristi Yamaguchi
figure skater
Her family is from _____.

Dan Aykroyd
actor/comedian/singer
Born in Canada.

Mikhail Baryshnikov
dancer
Born in _____.

A New Home

EPISODE **12**

THEMES
- Living in a Boarding House
- Cultural Differences
- Growing Old

INFORMATION GAP
- Paying Bills

OPTIONAL PROJECT
- Retirement Homes (Appendix 12)

THEME **Living in a Boarding House**

1 **PARTNER** **INTERVIEW**

partner's name

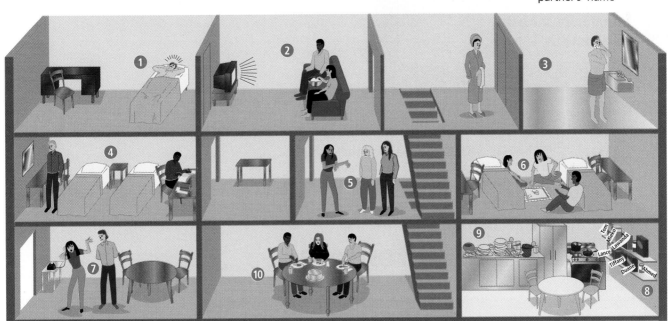

Imagine that you live in a boarding house like Nancy's. What would you like about living there? What would you dislike?

A. Look at the picture and the list of activities. Write *L* next to the things you would *like*, and *D* next to the things you would *dislike*.

B. Compare your answers with those of a partner. If any of your answers are different, ask this question: *Why would you like/dislike that?* Explain the reason for your answer.

_____ hearing loud noises

_____ watching TV together

_____ waiting for the bathroom

_____ having a roommate

_____ talking with others

_____ playing games

_____ sharing a telephone

_____ putting your name on food

_____ cleaning up

_____ eating meals together

Nancy Shaw's boarding house has three rules: no smoking, no drugs, no guests upstairs. Could you live with these rules? Discuss the rules below with the people in your group. Choose *five* rules that you can *all* agree to live with. Write them on the lines below.

HOUSE RULES

- lights out at 10 p.m.
- no loud music
- no guests upstairs
- 10-minute telephone calls
- no smoking
- no drugs
- no cooking after 9 p.m.
- no drinking alcohol
- put your name on all food
- clean up your mess
- 3-minute showers
- be home by 11 p.m.

Our group's rules

1. _____
2. _____
3. _____
4. _____
5. _____

What About YOU?

1. Which do you prefer, living alone or with other people?
2. Do you think it's easy to have a roommate?
3. What's a rule you would make if you had a boarding house?

THEME Cultural Differences

Look at the list of things below that Rebecca and her friends do.

A. Put an **X** next to the things that *do not* happen in your country. Put a ✔ next to the things that *do* happen in your country.

B. Get into groups and compare your **X**s and ✔s. If you have different answers from those of your group members, ask this question: *Why does/doesn't that happen in your country?*

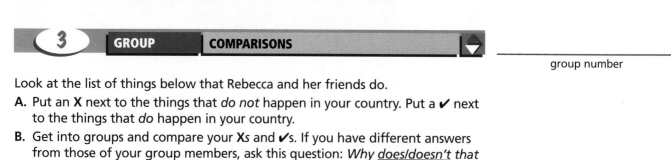

- _____ play on sports teams
- _____ have between two and four children
- _____ choose your own friends

- _____ leave home before getting married
- _____ live with a boyfriend or girlfriend
- _____ keep a diary

- _____ go far away to college
- _____ travel alone
- _____ don't marry until late 20's or older

People from different places live together in Nancy's boarding house. Here are some expressions to use when you are visiting another country or someone else's home for the first time:

> **Is it OK if** I sleep late?
>
> **Do you mind if** I watch television?
>
> **Is it all right if** I take your picture?
>
> **Is it a problem if** I smoke in here ?

Work with a partner. Look at the situations below. Take turns. One person chooses a situation. The other person uses one of the expressions from above. Then, make up your own situations.

	Situations	**Expressions**
EXAMPLE	You want to have something to eat.	Is it all right if I have something to eat?
1.	You want to take off your shoes.	
2.	You want to use the telephone.	
3.	You want to listen to some music.	
4.	You want to have something to drink.	
5.	You want to sit down.	
6.	You want to invite a friend to the house.	
7.	Your situation:	
8.	Your partner's situation:	

1. Do you have any friends or family from another country?
2. Would you marry someone from a different country?
3. Do you think it's hard or easy to live in a different country?
4. What's the most difficult part of living in a different country?

5 | **PARTNER** | **SHARING**

_____
partner's name

Uncle Edward is a very important person in Nancy Shaw's life. Do you have a special older person in your life? Be ready to tell your partner about this person.

Step One

Ask each other the questions below. They are about a special older person.
Write what your partner says.

1. What is the person's name?

2. Is she/he a relative?

3. How often do you see this person?

4. What do you do when you're with this person?

5. Do you take care of this person?

6. Where does he/she live?

7. What do you like best about him/her?

8. What are three words that describe him/her?

9. Your own question:

Step Two

Write a short paragraph about the person your partner described.

Step Three

When you're done writing, read what you have written to your partner.
Your partner will tell you if you have understood everything correctly.

INFORMATION GAP **Paying Bills**

partner's name

STUDENT A Work with a partner. One of you works on this page. The other works on page 6. Don't look at your partner's page!

What are Nancy and Rebecca's bills each month? Work with your partner to find out what Nancy and Rebecca have to pay.

A. Ask your partner questions about the missing information on your page.

EXAMPLE How much does Rebecca have to pay for <u>food</u>?

B. Write the amounts in the empty spaces. Then, add up the total amount and write it at the bottom.

C. Look at the totals with your partner. Who spends more on bills each month—Rebecca or Nancy?

MONTHLY EXPENSES

Rebecca's bills	Amount	Nancy's bills	Amount
rent	$250	taxes/insurance	$500
telephone		gas, electric, and telephone	$450
food		food	
entertainment	$50	entertainment	
college tuition and books		Uncle Edward's retirement home	$2,000
transportation	$50	gas for car	
miscellaneous (laundry, stamps, snacks)		miscellaneous (repairs, household items)	$100
TOTAL	$	TOTAL	$

D. Is there anything missing from the chart? Make a list with your partner of any other bills that Rebecca and Nancy might have to pay this month.

_____   _____
_____   _____
_____   _____
_____   _____
_____   _____

 Ask your partner these questions:
1. Do you have to pay a lot of bills each month?
2. What is your most expensive bill?
3. What is your least expensive bill?

INFORMATION GAP **Paying Bills**

6 **PARTNER** **INFORMATION GAP**

partner's name

STUDENT B Work with a partner. One of you works on this page. The other works on page 5. Don't look at your partner's page!

What are Nancy and Rebecca's bills each month? Work with your partner to find out what Nancy and Rebecca have to pay.

A. Ask your partner questions about the missing information on your page.

EXAMPLE How much does Nancy have to pay for <u>gas, electric, and telephone</u>?

B. Write the amounts in the empty spaces. Then, add up the total amount and write it at the bottom.

C. Look at the totals with your partner. Who spends more on bills each month—Rebecca or Nancy?

MONTHLY EXPENSES

Rebecca's bills	Amount	Nancy's bills	Amount
rent		taxes/insurance	
telephone	$60	gas, electric, and telephone	
food	$150	food	$240
entertainment		entertainment	$100
college tuition and books	$1,200	Uncle Edward's retirement home	
transportation		gas for car	$70
miscellaneous (laundry, stamps, snacks)	$20	miscellaneous (repairs, household items)	
TOTAL	$	TOTAL	$

D. Is there anything missing from the chart? Make a list with your partner of any other bills that Rebecca and Nancy might have to pay this month.

_____   _____

_____   _____

_____   _____

_____   _____

_____   _____

Ask your partner these questions:
1. Do you have to pay a lot of bills each month?
2. What is your most expensive bill?
3. What is your least expensive bill?

EPISODE 1

PROJECT **Choosing a College**

---

1   **PARTNER**   **RANKING** ▲

_____
partner's name

There are many reasons for choosing a college or university. Which reasons are most important to *you*? Number them from 1 to 9, with 1 as the most important.

_____ class size   _____ help with job placement

_____ location   _____ courses offered

_____ quality of teachers   _____ quality of ESL/ EFL classes

_____ scholarships   _____ facilities (library, labs, and so on)

_____ cost

Compare answers with your partner. Do you have the same number 1 reason? On a separate sheet of paper, write a list of other things that are important in choosing a college or university.

---

2   **TEAM**   **PRESENTATION** ⬍

_____
team number

Divide into four teams. Teams 1, 2, and 3 will each research a different local college or university and present their information to the rest of the class. Team 4 will decide which school to go to, based on the presentations by the other three teams.

Teams 1, 2, and 3

A. Go to the library and get as much information as possible about your college or university. You can also use the Internet or call or visit the Admissions Office. Ask someone who works there to send you a catalog or a brochure.

B. After reviewing all of your information, choose five advantages (positive things) about your school. Write them on a separate piece of paper. (*Example: The Boston School of Music offers over 75 different music classes to students.*)

C. Prepare and practice your presentation. You can also make a written handout of your information for Team 4.

Team 4

Listen carefully as each team gives its presentation. On a separate piece of paper, make three copies of the chart on the right. As each team makes its presentation, write the advantages it mentions. Then, as a team, discuss the three presentations. Choose the college you want to go to. Make your choice based on the answers to these questions:
- *Which team had the most useful information?*
- *Which team had the most convincing presentation?*
- *Which team had the best written material?*

After you have made your choice, tell all of the teams which college you want to go to, and why.

Team # _____

College _____

Advantages

1. _____

2. _____

3. _____

4. _____

5. _____

EPISODE 2

PROJECT **Working in a Factory**

1 GROUP RESEARCH

group number

In this episode, Rebecca and Sandy are working in a computer factory. Divide into groups and find out about factories in or near the area where you live. Complete the information below. You may use your school library, a telephone book, the Internet, or any other source of information.

1. List at least three factories in your area.

2. List at least three products made in your area.

3. In your opinion, what is the most important factory-based industry in your area?

2 GROUP FACTORY INTERVIEW

group number

A. Choose one of the factories that you listed in Activity 1. Interview someone who works there. Invite this person to speak to your class, or visit the factory for a tour.

B. Find out as much as you can about the factory. Ask the questions below. Write the answers on a separate sheet of paper.
   1. What's the name of the company/factory?
   2. What's the name of the person telling your class about the factory?
   3. What's his/her job at the factory?
   4. How many people work there?
   5. What products do they make there?
   6. How many years has the company been in business?
   7. How do they make their products?
   8. What's the most interesting thing about the factory?

1. Have you ever worked in a factory?
2. If yes, what did you like about your job? What didn't you like?
3. If no, would you like to work in a factory? Why or why not?
4. Are factory conditions in your country generally good?

EPISODE 3

PROJECT Holidays

 GROUP **RESEARCH**

What do you know about American holidays?

A. Divide into groups. Each group chooses a different holiday from the list.

B. Find out everything you can about the holiday. Use an encyclopedia, the Internet, or books from the library.

C. Answer the questions below about your holiday. Write your answers on a separate sheet of paper.

D. Present your information to the class. If you want, your group can create a poster about your holiday.

- Valentine's Day
- Memorial Day
- July 4th
- Labor Day
- Halloween
- Thanksgiving
- Christmas

Our Holiday

1. When is your holiday?
2. Why is it a holiday?
3. What do people do on this holiday?
4. What is something interesting or unusual about this holiday?
5. What do you like about this holiday?

 GROUP **RESEARCH**

Divide into groups. Work with your group to find a holiday for every month of the year. You can use holidays from different parts of the world, but don't use any holidays from Activity 1 above.

A. Look for information in calendars, the library, or on the Internet. Interview people you know.

B. Copy the chart below onto a separate piece of paper. In the chart, fill in the information about each holiday. Write the name of the holiday, the country where it is celebrated, and the day it is celebrated. Write one sentence about what people do on this holiday.

C. Compare charts with another group. Did you have any of the same holidays? Tell the other groups about any holidays that they do not have in their chart.

	JANUARY	FEBRUARY	MARCH	APRIL	MAY	JUNE
Name:						
Country:						
Day:						
What people do:						

	JULY	AUGUST	SEPTEMBER	OCTOBER	NOVEMBER	DECEMBER
Name:						
Country:						
Day:						
What people do:						

EPISODE 4

PROJECT **Being Proud**

  PARTNER | **SURVEY**

_____
partner's name

Work with a partner. Find two people to interview outside of class. Take turns asking the questions below and writing the answers in the chart.

	PERSON 1	PERSON 2
Is there a friend you are proud of? Why are you proud of him/her?	The friend: Why you are proud:	The friend: Why you are proud:
Is there a family member you are proud of? Why are you proud of him/her?	The family member: Why you are proud:	The family member: Why you are proud:
Is there someone from your country you are proud of? Why are you proud of him/her?	The person from your country: Why you are proud:	The person from your country: Why you are proud:
Is there something about your hometown that makes you proud? What is it?	What: Why you are proud:	What: Why you are proud:
Is there something about your country that makes you proud? What is it?	What: Why you are proud:	What: Why you are proud:

  PARTNER | **WRITING**

_____
partner's name

Look at the survey above. Which answer is the most interesting?

A. With your partner, decide which answer you both like the best.

B. Working together, write a short paragraph about the answer. Tell _who_ or _what_ the person is proud of, and _why_ that person is proud.

C. Copy your paragraph onto a clean sheet of paper, and post it on the bulletin board in your classroom.

D. With your classmates, decide on a title for the bulletin board.

EPISODE 5

PROJECT **Shopping for Clothes**

 PARTNER **CONSUMER RESEARCH**

_____
partner's name

Imagine that you're invited to a formal party, and you need to buy all of your clothes—everything "from head to toe." Visit some clothing stores with your partner, or look in a newspaper or some clothing catalogs.

A. Find out what it would cost to look your *best*. Write the items and the costs under "The Best."

B. Then, figure out the *cheapest* possible outfit. Write those items and the costs under "The Cheapest."

C. Write the names of the stores you went to.

D. Compare charts with another pair.

Who spent the most?

Who spent the least?

In general, did the women have to pay more for their items than the men?

THE BEST		THE CHEAPEST	
Item	Cost	Item	Cost
1.		1.	
2.		2.	
3.		3.	
4.		4.	
5.		5.	
TOTAL:		TOTAL:	
Store/s:		Store/s:	

 PARTNER **RESEARCH**

_____
partner's name

In this episode, Rebecca spends $60.00 on her dress.

A. Use the financial section of a newspaper to find out how much this would cost in the currency of your country. Write your answers in line 1 below, and check () whether Rebecca's dress would be considered expensive, reasonable, or cheap in your country. If your partner is from a different country, write his/her answers in line 2 of the chart.

B. Discuss your answers as a class. If there are people from other countries in your class, write down their answers in the extra lines in the chart.

Country	Currency	Cost in country's currency	Expensive	Reasonable	Cheap
1.					
2.					
3.					
4.					

EPISODE 6

PROJECT **The Boston Red Sox**

partner's name

Rebecca's friends give her a Red Sox jacket as a good-bye present. The Red Sox are the professional baseball team in Boston, Massachusetts. In the United States and Canada, professional baseball teams are organized in two major leagues: the *National League* and the *American League*. (A **league** is a group of teams.)

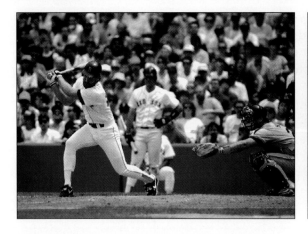

A. Work in pairs. One person will get information about the *National League*. The other person will get information about the *American League*.

B. Answer the questions below about your league. Use your school or public library, an encyclopedia, or the Internet. Write the answers on a separate piece of paper.

   1. How many teams are in the <u>American/National</u> League?

   2. How many divisions are there in this league?

   3. What are the names of these divisions?

   4. What are the names of the teams in each division? List them under each division.

   5. Which teams are familiar to you?

C. When you finish, compare the two leagues. How are they the same? How are they different?

group number

A. Divide into groups. Each group chooses a different professional baseball team.

B. Complete the information below about your team. Use your school or public library, an almanac, an encyclopedia, or the Internet.

C. Bring in pictures of your team or some players. Choose a volunteer from your group to present your information to the class.

Team name _____

Best batter(s) _____

Best pitcher(s) _____

Number of games won last year _____

Other interesting information _____

EPISODE

PROJECT **Discovering the United States**

group number

A. Divide into groups. Each group chooses a different region of the U.S. and writes the names of the states in their region on the map below.

B. The whole class will make one large map on a poster board. One person from each group will write the names of the states from their region on the class map.

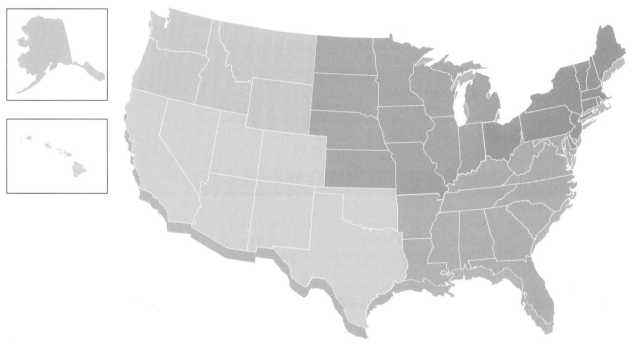

2 GROUP STATE RESEARCH

group number

Work in your group from Activity 1. Choose one state in your region. Complete the information below about your state. You can use your school library, a dictionary, an almanac, an encyclopedia, the Internet, and so on. Present your information to the class.

Our state _____

Population _____

Largest cities _____

Tourist attractions _____

Other interesting information _____

1. Who is your favorite celebrity from the U.S.?
2. What state is that person from?
3. Why is your celebrity famous?
4. What do you like about that person?

EPISODE 8

PROJECT **The Desert**

1 | **GROUP** | **RESEARCH**

In this episode, Rebecca drives through a desert in the southwestern part of the United States. What do you know about deserts? Divide into groups. Answer the questions below. You can use an encyclopedia, atlas, almanac, or the Internet to find the information.

1. What is a desert? _____

_____

2. Which is the largest desert in the world? _____

_____

3. List some other large deserts and their locations. _____

_____

2 | **GROUP** | **RESEARCH**

Divide into groups. Using an encyclopedia and other books, find out about desert life and landscape. Then draw a picture below (or on a larger sheet of paper) of a desert. Label all the plants, animals, and other things your group decides to draw. Present your information to the class.

 **What About YOU?**
1. Have you ever been to or lived in a desert?
2. Have you ever driven across a desert?
3. Do you like hot, dry weather?

EPISODE 9

PROJECT **Staying in a Motel**

1 **PARTNER** **RESEARCH**

partner's name

A. Work with a partner. Answer the questions below. Use a dictionary or a travel guide to find the answers to questions 1 and 2. Use your own paper.

1. What's a motel?

2. What's a hotel?

3. What's the difference between a motel and a hotel?

4. Is the Star Lite Lodge a motel or a hotel?

B. Each group will find a different motel or hotel to call or visit. Tell the receptionist that you're doing a project for your English class. Ask the receptionist the questions below, and write your answers.

1. What's the name of the motel/hotel? _____

2. How many rooms does it have? _____

3. What's the rate for a single room? _____

4. What's the rate for a double room? _____

5. Does it have a pool? _____

6. Does it have an exercise room? _____

7. Does it have a restaurant? _____

8. Does it have a conference room? _____

2 **GROUP** **COMPARISONS**

group number

Divide into groups. Join a different group from that of your partner from Activity 1. Look at the information above. Compare motels/hotels with your group.

1. Which motel/hotel has the most rooms? _____

2. Which motel/hotel is the most expensive? _____

3. Which motel/hotel is the cheapest? _____

4. Which motels/hotels have a pool? _____

5. Which motels/hotels have an exercise room? _____

6. Which motels/hotels have a restaurant? _____

7. Which motels/hotels have a conference room? _____

8. Which motel/hotel is the best value overall? _____

EPISODE 10

PROJECT Native Americans

1 **GROUP** **RESEARCH**

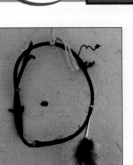

In this episode, Rebecca and Alberto look at a Native American dream catcher.

A. Divide into five groups. Each group takes a different question from the list below.

B. Find out the answer to your question about Native Americans (American Indians). Use your school library, an encyclopedia, the Internet, and so on. Write your answers on a separate piece of paper.

C. Each group will present its information to the class. Draw pictures or maps for your presentations.

   1. What is a Native American?

   2. What is a Native American *tribe*? Name at least three different tribes. What language does each tribe speak?

3. What are some differences among Native American tribes?

4. What is a Native American *reservation*? Give the locations of three reservations.

5. Many Native Americans make beautiful crafts representing their cultures. They make things with their hands, like the dream catcher. They also make other things like jewelry. Name two other things that Native Americans make.

2 **CLASS** **DISCUSSION**

Dreams are very important in many Native American cultures. As a class, discuss the following questions about the importance of dreams.

1. Are dreams important in your culture?

2. Do you think dreams can tell about the future?

3. Do you think the dream catcher works?

4. Is there something in your culture like a dream catcher?

Take a vote in your class.

How many people think the dream catcher would work? _____

How many don't think it would work? _____

How many people would like to try a dream catcher? _____

EPISODE **11**

PROJECT **Nature and Natural Beauty**

Pretend you have won a trip to a world-famous place of natural beauty.

A. Divide into groups. Your teacher will assign you one of the trips below.

B. Using the library, an encyclopedia, the Internet, and so on, research your destination for the information below.

C. Present your information to the rest of the class. Tell why you think your trip would be the most interesting.

1. The Grand Canyon National Park in the United States

Best time of the year to go _____

Things to see _____

Fun things to do _____

Interesting facts about this place _____

_____

2. The Galápagos Islands in Ecuador

Best time of the year to go _____

Things to see _____

Fun things to do _____

Interesting facts about this place _____

_____

3. The Masai Mara National Reserve in Kenya

Best time of the year to go _____

Things to see _____

Fun things to do _____

Interesting facts about this place _____

_____

4. The Great Barrier Reef Marine Park in Australia

Best time of the year to go _____

Things to see _____

Fun things to do _____

Interesting facts about this place _____

_____

1. Where is the most popular place of natural beauty in your country?
2. What is the most beautiful place you have ever been?
3. Do you enjoy hiking or camping?

EPISODE 12

PROJECT **Retirement Homes**

 1 **GROUP** **DISCUSSION**

group number

Nancy doesn't want her uncle Edward to live in a retirement home, but he must. Nancy can't take care of him anymore. Retirement homes are very common in the United States and Canada. When senior citizens (old people) can't live alone or need special help, they can move into a retirement home. Most people who live in retirement homes have their own apartments or rooms. Employees in a retirement home often plan activities or short trips for the senior citizens who live there. Many times, there are also doctors, nurses, and counselors who work in retirement homes.

Answer these questions, and then discuss your answers with the people in your group.

1. Are there retirement homes where you live? _____
2. If there aren't, where do most older people live? _____
3. Have you ever been to a retirement home? _____
4. What do you think of retirement homes? _____

 2 **GROUP** **SURVEY**

group number

Read the questions in the chart below about retirement homes. Interview two people outside of class and check (✔) their responses.

Step One
Introduce your survey like this:

I'm doing a survey. It's about retirement homes.

Would you answer some questions?

Step Two
Explain what a retirement home is. Either let the person read the information in Activity 1, or describe a retirement home in your own words.

Step Three
Start the survey like this:

I'll read a sentence.

Please answer *Yes* or *No*.

Step Four
After you've completed the survey, meet with your group from Activity 1. Share your information. Answer this question: *Do most people think retirement homes are good or bad places?*

	Person 1		Person 2	
	Yes	No	Yes	No
1. I've visited a retirement home.				
2. I think retirement homes are good places to live.				
3. I think old people should live with other people their own age.				
4. I would put my parents or older relatives in a retirement home.				
5. I would like to live in a retirement home.				
6. I would not like to live in a retirement home.				

APPENDIX 13 Manipulatives

Episode 7

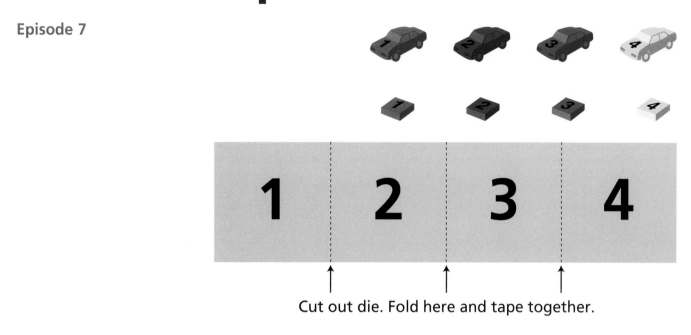

Cut out die. Fold here and tape together.

Episode 10

A MUFFLER	A TIRE	A HEADLIGHT	A FAN BELT
A BATTERY	A FUEL PUMP	BRAKE PADS	A RADIATOR
SPARK PLUGS	AN AIR FILTER	A TAILPIPE	A FRONT BUMPER
A CARBURETOR	SPARK PLUG WIRES	A RADIATOR HOSE	SHOCK ABSORBERS